Georgian and
Regency Conservatories:
History, design and conservation

Georgian and Regency Conservatories:

History, design and conservation

Melissa Thompson and
Michael Borozdin-Bidnell

Published by Historic England, The Engine House, Fire Fly Avenue, Swindon SN2 2EH
www.HistoricEngland.org.uk

Historic England is a Government service championing England's heritage and giving expert, constructive advice.

The views expressed in this book are those of the authors and not necessarily those of Historic England.

First published 2019

ISBN 978-1-84802-282-9

British Library Cataloguing in Publication data
A CIP catalogue record for this book is available from the British Library.

For more information about images from the Archive, contact Archives Services Team, Historic England, The Engine House, Fire Fly Avenue, Swindon SN2 2EH; telephone (01793) 414600.

Brought to publication by Sarah Enticknap Publishing, Historic England.

Typeset in Georgia Pro 9/11pt

Edited by Kathleen Steeden
Indexed by Caroline Jones, Osprey Indexing
Page layout by Matthew Wilson

Printed in the UK by Gomer Press

Front cover: The conservatory at The Deepdene, Surrey, in 1823. [© London Borough of Lambeth Archive]

Frontispiece: The conservatory at Shrubland Park, Suffolk. [© Historic England Archive BB99/06188]

Contents

Part 2:
Subsequent developments to conservatories
and glasshouses and conservation approaches

Acknowledgements

The authors wish to thank Tony Calladine and Sarah Gibson of Historic England, and the staff at the British Library. They are indebted to John Wallis (Dorothea Restorations), Geoff Wallis CEng MIMechE and Robert Jameson (Foster and Pearson) for their generous advice, time and permission to use information from their notes for the compilation of this text. They are also grateful to the architects and consultants, and their very helpful staff, who allowed use of their materials for the case studies, especially Christopher Garrand (Christopher Garrand Consultancy – Architect), Robin Dower (Spence and Dower, Chartered Architects and Historic Building Consultants), John Tiernan (Historic England), David Johnson (Dannatt, Johnson Architects), Donald Insall (Donald Insall Associates), Hugh Petter (ADAM Architecture), Eric Watts (Martin Ashley Architects), Chris Dyson (Chris Dyson Architects). Thanks are also due to Andrew Fuller for allowing the use of images from his extensive collection of photographs of conservatories and glasshouses.

1 | The emergence of the conservatory

Introduction

The earliest structures designed to cultivate and protect exotic fruits and plants appeared in England in the 17th century. Owing to the cost of their maintenance, orangeries or hothouses, as they were usually called, were for centuries the preserve of the very wealthy, who regarded them as a mark of their elevated social status. In the early 19th century, however, the increased interest in horticulture as well as developments in glass and iron manufacture, and in methods of heating, brought the greenhouse within the reach of the middle classes for the first time. It began increasingly to be attached to the house in order to be used as a social space and came to be known more consistently as a conservatory. Now a sought-after appendage to a house, the desire for the new fashion is aptly illustrated in a scene from Benjamin Disraeli's novel *Henrietta Temple* (1837) in which the heroine's father says, 'I built a conservatory, to be sure. Henrietta could not do without a conservatory'; to which Ferdinand replies, 'Miss Temple is quite right, it is impossible to live without a conservatory.'[1]

First introduced by Humphry Repton (1752–1818) in his designs for country estates, the conservatory was then advocated by John Claudius Loudon (1783–1843), who contributed more than anyone else to increasing its accessibility to households lower down the social scale. As he commented in 1832, 'a green-house, which fifty years ago, was a luxury not often to be met with, is now become an appendage to every villa, and to many town residences.'[2] Loudon is a towering figure in the horticultural world of the late Georgian and early Victorian period and, as so many of the smaller conservatories attached to villas and more modest houses have been lost, his designs and specifications – along with those of other figures such as John Papworth (1775–1847) and George Tod (dates unknown) – provide invaluable evidence of what is now a relatively rare building type.

The purpose of this book is twofold. First, it shows how and why the conservatory emerged in the form it did in the early 19th century. Drawing on contemporary architects' plans, horticultural publications, diaries and memoirs, Part 1 explores why conservatories were positioned adjacent to certain rooms in the house, who built them, what they were like inside and how they were used by their owners.

The principal materials of conservatories – iron, glass and timber, along with their various surface coatings – have all been subject to deterioration over the years. Corrosion, fluctuating thermal environments, mechanical shocks, original manufacturing defects, as well as poorly designed or executed alterations and repairs, or even straightforward lack of care and maintenance, have all played a role in the deterioration of these vulnerable structures.

The second purpose of this book, therefore, is to explore ways in which the various elements of conservatories may be conserved. Part 2 will look at the ways in which the materials and components of these often forgotten, but nonetheless architecturally and culturally significant structures, have deteriorated, as well as the various methods and approaches used in their conservation. Part 2 is divided into five sections, with specific case studies highlighting practical approaches to the conservation and repair of metalwork, glazing, woodwork and surface coatings, as well as the importance of recording and storage. It is hoped that this study will offer practical guidance for practitioners, architects, owners and those involved in the heritage industry.

The origins of the conservatory

The most refined enjoyments of society have generally arisen from desires more simple, and even from wants. Man is fond of living beings, and after assembling those plants around him which he found necessary for food, he would select such as were agreeable to the eye, or fragrant to the smell. ... Tender rare plants in pots would be taken into the house for shelter, and set near the window for light, and hence the origin of the Green-house. ... A taste for this appendage to a dwelling is natural to man; to experience that it adds to his enjoyments; and to feel that it bestows a certain claim to distinction on its possessor.[3]

The cultivation of exotic plants, particularly oranges, was for centuries restricted to households in the highest social sphere. In Tudor England it is likely that they would have been grown in tubs and displayed in the garden in the summer months, then placed indoors or in outhouses during cold weather, as there is no evidence to suggest that any masonry structures were specifically built for orange trees. One of the earliest known purpose-built orangeries in Britain was erected in the 1630s for Queen Henrietta Maria at Wimbledon Manor House (Fig 1). It was a single-storey brick building with full-height windows along the front and a slate-clad roof lit by dormer windows, as the dormant trees would not have needed much overhead sunlight.

By the mid-17th century orangeries were usually heated by an open fire or a free-standing iron stove, fuelled by charcoal, coal or wood, with a flue in the floor or back wall. These methods of heating were not easy to regulate and could give off noxious fumes which were detrimental to the health of the plants. A cheaper alternative was piling up dung and other warmth-giving composting materials against the wall. In 1664 John Evelyn (1620–1706), the diarist, gardener and founder member of the Royal Society, suggested placing the stove

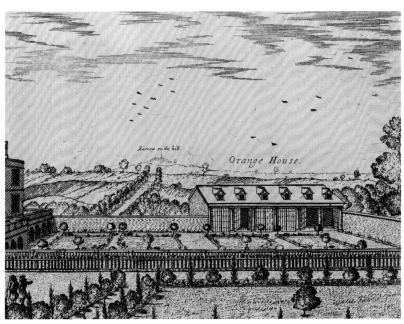

Fig 1
The 'Orange House', erected in the 1630s for Queen Henrietta Maria at Wimbledon Manor House, here seen in a print made by Henry Winstanley (1678–90). [© British Museum]

outside the orangery and using pipes to transfer the heat inside. Twenty years later a system was invented by John Watts (dates unknown), Gardener to the Society of Apothecaries, that conveyed heat under the floor of the orangery. By the 1710s the new orangery built for the Duke of Chandos at Cannons, in Little Stanmore, Middlesex, was heated by flues running in from the end walls, which also had coal fireplaces.

The first orangery to be built adjoining a house was probably that at Hampton Court Palace designed by Sir Christopher Wren (1632–1723) for William and Mary in the 1690s. This created a new fashion at royal residences and country estates, where the most sought-after architects of the 18th century, such as Robert Adam (1728–92), Capability Brown (1716–83) and Sir William Chambers (1723–96), were commissioned. Notable early examples include the adjoining orangery designed by William Talman (1650–1719) for William Blathwayt at Dyrham Park, Gloucestershire (1701) (Fig 2); the baroque orangery designed by Nicholas Hawksmoor (1661–1736) for Queen Anne at Kensington Palace (1704); and the orangery at Blenheim Palace, Oxfordshire (1705), designed by Sir John Vanbrugh (1664–1726). Such grand buildings as these were conceived not just as horticultural structures but as architectural showpieces to be used for banquets, theatrical productions and other social entertainments, especially when the plants had been taken outside during the summer or into the house when in full bloom.

The majority of orangeries were designed in the prevailing classical style, such as that at Kenwood House beside Hampstead Heath, London, which was remodelled between 1764 and 1779 by Robert Adam for the 1st Earl of Mansfield (Fig 3). Repton observed that they mostly harmonised with the architectural character of the house, hence Capability Brown's unusual Gothic creation at Burghley House near Stamford, Lincolnshire, which adjoined the house and faced onto a sheltered courtyard with views of the grounds beyond (Fig 4). Most orangeries of this period were free-standing as, by the end of the

Fig 2

The adjoining orangery designed by William Talman for William Blathwayt at Dyrham Park, Gloucestershire (1701).

[© Historic England Archive P/G00598/004]

Fig 3
The orangery at Kenwood
House in Hampstead, London,
remodelled between 1764 and
1779 by Robert Adam for the first
Earl of Mansfield. [© Historic
England Archive DP035028]

century, the fashion for attaching them to the house had subsided under the influence of the landscape movement, which favoured naturalistic grounds around the house rather than formally laid out gardens.

The botanist Dr Richard Bradley, FRS, had published a design for an orangery with a partially glazed roof back in 1718, but generally 18th-century orangeries continued to have solid roofs as well as piers that could be almost as wide as the windows. They were admired more for their elaborate architectural qualities than their horticultural function, but this was set to change in the first decades of the 19th century.

Fig 4
Capability Brown's orangery at
Burghley House near Stamford,
Lincolnshire. The corner turrets
echo those of the flamboyant
Elizabethan house. [© Paul Belford]

The emergence of the conservatory

There can be no stronger argument in favour of this method of growing plants, than the numerous buildings of this kind that have lately been erected by the nobility and gentry throughout the kingdom; and the practice being patronized, and recommended by men of the first respectability among gardeners, who have either through inclination or necessity dedicated a considerable part of their time to the study of natural knowledge: also the self-evident utility and pleasure accruing therefrom renders it partly unnecessary for me to attempt saying any thing in its favour.[4]

The definition of a conservatory

John Evelyn is credited with being the first, in 1664, to use the term 'conservatory', by which he meant a place for conserving delicate plants over the winter months.[5] He employed the term 'greenhouse' in the same way, and this usage continued throughout the 18th century. In 1785 the novelist and courtier Fanny Burney (1752–1840) recorded that Queen Charlotte asked her if she had lately been at Mrs Walsingham's. The queen remarks that 'it is a pretty place', and asks, 'has not she lately made some improvements?', to which Fanny Burney replies, 'Yes, ma'am; she has built a conservatory.'[6] By the early 19th century the terms conservatory and greenhouse were still being used interchangeably by Repton but a distinction in their meaning was becoming apparent. 'Greenhouse' came to denote the structure used for potting plants and overwintering, whereas 'conservatory' was used to describe a structure, usually attached to the house, in which planted beds were growing permanently. Greenhouses had glazed roofs, as opposed to orangeries, which invariably had solid roofs. Conservatories were often treated architecturally to harmonise with the house, whereas greenhouses, which had a practical rather than a social function, were usually detached structures of more modest design.

In 1812 the hothouse builder and surveyor George Tod still used both terms without any apparent distinction when referring to his designs for horticultural structures that adjoined the house.[7] A few years later the architect and landscape designer John Papworth (1775–1847) stated that 'the conservatory is distinguished from the greenhouse by the circumstances of its affording protection only to the plants; whereas the latter is used for rearing them, and it has become an apartment in which they are arranged for display, merely allowing space for walks or a promenade, and is frequently used as a breakfast or dining room.'[8] By 1835 Loudon defined conservatories as 'plant-houses, in which the plants are grown in a bed or border without the use of pots. They are sometimes placed in the pleasure-ground along with the other hot-houses, but more frequently attached to the mansion.'[9] His wife, the botanical writer Jane Loudon (1807–58), added that by putting the plants in the free soil they are allowed to assume their natural shapes and habits of growth.[10] Conservatories therefore contained large or fine specimens, while plants in greenhouses would be kept quite small and young by repeated propagation.

Fashionable horticultural pursuits

By the early 19th century, the popularity of exotic plants requiring shelter and warmth all year round stimulated experiments to find the most efficacious design for a greenhouse. As Loudon pointed out in 1806, their construction was still 'very imperfectly understood among those who are generally employed to erect them', which was not surprising considering 'how very recently they have become general in gentlemen's gardens'.[11] The vogue for collecting plants had gathered pace throughout the 18th century, so that by 1812 Tod observed how 'botany, an elegant and interesting study, has lately become a favourite pursuit among the higher classes of the community; and the attention to forcing of plants, flowers, and fruits, for the table, has increased the demand for Horticultural Buildings of every description.'[12]

During the Georgian period the number of plants cultivated in Britain increased from 1,000 to 5,000, and the number of nurseries in London rose from 15 to 200.[13] The plant trade flourished as a result of the canal network and road improvements, and especially after the invention of the Wardian case by Nathaniel Bagshaw Ward (1791–1868) in 1832, which enabled the successful transportation of specimens over long distances. Horticultural societies were founded and botanical publications ran into many editions. The Royal Botanic Gardens at Kew were established in 1759, becoming a significant international centre for the distribution of plants when Sir Joseph Banks took over as director in 1771; and what was to become the Royal Horticultural Society was founded in 1801. The highly influential *Gardener's Dictionary* by Philip Miller was published between 1731 and 1768, and went into eight editions in his lifetime; and Loudon's numerous publications, notably *An Encyclopaedia of Gardening* (1822) and *The Gardener's Magazine*, established in 1826, were hugely popular.

Technological innovations

The development of glass roofs
One of the most significant developments in the design of conservatories was the invention of the glazed roof. Until the turn of the 19th century, the roofs of glasshouses had usually been covered in slate or other traditional roofing materials. The new design stemmed from the realisation that imported exotics required year-round protection and benefited from more overhead light. Repton observed in 1803 that 'the numerous tribe of geraniums, ericas and other exotic plants, requiring more light, have caused a very material alteration in the construction of the green-house; and, perhaps, the more it resembles the shape of a nurseryman's stove, the better it will be adapted to the purposes of the modern green-house.'[14] The late 18th-century orangery at Barton Seagrave Hall in Northamptonshire, with its partially glazed dome roof, marks a transitional stage in the evolution of buildings allowing in more light (Fig 5). It is thought that greenhouses with fully glazed roofs may actually have been built as early as the 1790s, but one of the earliest surviving examples is at Chiselhampton House, Oxfordshire, which was built *c* 1800. The five-sided cast-iron structure leans against a stone wall and has an angled roof with small scalloped glazing with short, straight glazing bars (Fig 6).[15]

The creation of the curvilinear iron glasshouse
The revolution in the design of glasshouses, which had hitherto taken the general form of a glazed shed or lean-to, is attributed to the horticulturalist Sir George Mackenzie in 1815. He realised that 'if a form for the glass can be found,

Fig 5
The partially glazed dome roof on the late 18th-century conservatory at Barton Seagrave Hall, Northamptonshire. [© Historic England Archive DP165071]

Fig 6
One of the first greenhouses with a fully glazed roof, at Chiselhampton House, Oxfordshire, built c 1800. [© Country Life 812181]

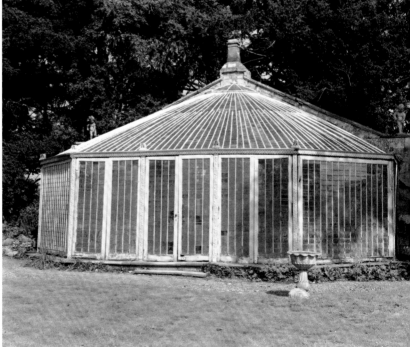

such that the rays will be perpendicular to *some part of it*, during the whole period of the sun's shining, not twice, but every day in the year, that form must be considered as the *ne plus ultra*.'[16]

The form he proposed was one-quarter of a sphere, or a semi-dome, supported by a wall. His illustration of the proposed design, which he believed had both neatness and elegance, shows that it is ventilated by sliding shutters at the base and along the top of the back wall, and heated by an underfloor flue leading to a chimney disguised as an urn (Fig 7). In response, Sir Thomas Andrew Knight (1759–1838), the esteemed botanist and president of the London Horticultural Society, agreed that the spherical form was ideal but

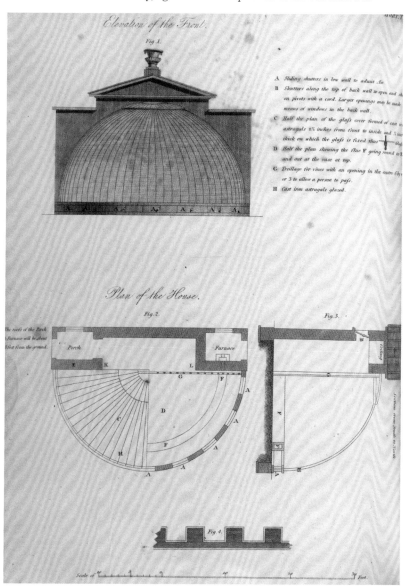

Fig 7

George Mackenzie's curvilinear design for a glasshouse (1815). [Reproduced by kind permission of the Syndics of Cambridge University Library (T439.b.36.2)]

offered some suggestions for the improvement of Mackenzie's design. He proposed a small segment of a much larger sphere and the reduction in the number of glazing bars by using iron wire to secure them.[17]

Loudon also regarded the hemispherical shape as the ultimate in regard to the principle and perfection of form. In 1816 he devised a wrought-iron glazing bar which could be curved in any direction without losing its strength, enabling Mackenzie's design to be constructed. Less brittle than cast iron, which is weak under tension, the wrought-iron bar could also be made more slender – just half an inch wide – which let in even more light. Loudon described his invention in *Remarks on the Construction of Hothouses* (1817) and *Sketches of Curvilinear Hothouses* (1818), which included an illustration of the first curvilinear iron-framed glasshouse in his own garden at Bayswater House in London (Fig 8).

He passed over the rights of production to the structural ironwork firm Messrs W and D Bailey of High Holborn, who subsequently achieved enormous success selling curvilinear iron-framed greenhouses and conservatories throughout the country. In addition to the horticultural advantages of constructing an iron-framed greenhouse, Loudon pointed out that wooden

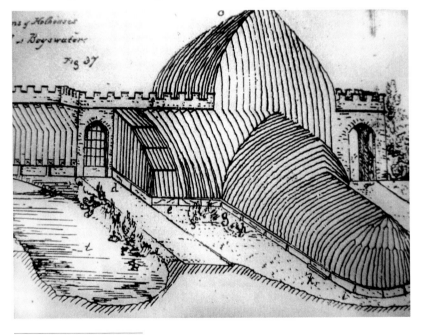

Fig 8
The first curvilinear iron-framed
glasshouse, constructed by John
Loudon in his own garden at
Bayswater House in London.
[© Royal Botanic Garden, Kew]

glazing bars soon rotted and continually warped so as to break the glass.[18] The argument over whether wood or iron sash bars were most suitable continued beyond the middle of the 19th century, however, with Sir Joseph Paxton (1803–65), the gardener and architect of the Great Stove at Chatsworth (1836–40), advocating the former and Loudon the latter.

Decimus Burton (1800–81) was one of the first architects to include spherical iron-framed conservatories in his designs for dwellings. In around 1818, when he was just 16, he designed The Holme in Regent's Park for his father. This Graeco-Roman villa was arranged internally as an enfilade terminating in a small polygonal conservatory opening off the dining room. Despite its modest scale, this conservatory was recognised as being one of the earliest structures to use the newly invented curved wrought-iron glazing bar for the roof and walls.[19] Burton's design for Grove Lodge (1822–24) in Regent's Park for George Bellas Greenough, a fellow of the Linnean Society, also included a curvilinear structure. Situated in the grounds, the conservatory is a segment of an elliptical sphere built against a screen wall, inspired directly by Mackenzie's proposed design (Fig 9). Another example of the lean-to, semi-dome form is the early 19th-century greenhouse built in the

Fig 9
Decimus Burton's curvilinear conservatory at Grove House in Regent's Park, London.
[© Steven Parissien]

Fig 10
The early 19th-century
greenhouse built in the grounds of
East Cliff Lodge (now the George
VI Memorial Park) in Ramsgate,
Kent. [© C Sebag-Montefiore]

grounds of East Cliff Lodge (now the George VI Memorial Park) in Ramsgate, Kent (Fig 10). This has a panelled base wall and cast-iron curving ribs with copper glazing bars holding in place fish-scale glass panes.

Advances in heating systems

These new iron-framed conservatories were further improved by innovations in heating techniques. In the 18th century, glasshouses had been heated using stoves or coal-fired underfloor or wall flues, but these methods produced a dry heat as well as fumes which were often harmful to plants, and they required regular stoking. According to Loudon, the first application of steam to the heating of hothouses was attempted by Wakefield of Liverpool in 1788, and afterwards applied in the vault of a cucumber house at Knowle Park, near Liverpool, by Butler, the gardener to the Earl of Derby, in 1792.[20] In 1818 Papworth remarked that 'ingenious stoves and apparatus have been lately invented and used for the purpose of heating conservatories and green-houses by steam', and by the early 1820s there were several different systems in operation.[21]

The use of hot water for heating had actually been invented in 1777 by the Frenchman M Bonnemain as a way of keeping chickens' eggs warm, and was applied by his exiled countryman Count Chabannes to the heating of his house in 1816. In the same year he also installed a heating system at Sundridge Park, Kent. In 1826 the architect William Atkinson (1774/5–1839) developed a successful system for heating conservatories using hot water supplied through cast-iron piping. The boiler for heating the water was located underground or in a rear shed, and the hot water was then circulated in cast-iron pipes placed either along the front and sides of the conservatory or under the floor and then covered by iron grilles. All this meant that, for the first time, conservatories could be heated more evenly and with a more constant temperature, without any smoke or fumes. Another advantage was that the use of stone as a building material, with its heat-retaining qualities, could be entirely dispensed with in favour of iron and glass.

The manufacture of glass

The final major technical advancement to affect the design of conservatories occurred in the manufacture of glass. The widespread use of crown glass as a building material had hitherto been prohibitive due to its cost and the restricted size of panes. Between 1746 and 1845 glass was taxed by weight, so it was more cost-effective to produce thin sheets which were, as a consequence, too fragile to be made into large panes. The tax was halved in 1825 making glass more affordable. Then in 1832 the Chance Bros of Birmingham produced much larger sheets than had previously been achieved by using a new method of blowing cylinder glass. The sheets were 36in (0.9m) in length, which was at least 14in (0.4m) longer than was possible using crown glass. The colourless sheet glass, as it became known, did not protect the plants as well as the thick crown glass, which had a greenish tinge, so it became more important to shade them effectively. The use of sheet glass in buildings did not become widespread until the middle of the 19th century as a result of the removal of the glass tax in 1845 and the repeal of the window tax in 1851. With these changes the price of a conservatory came within the reach of many more householders.

The integration of the conservatory within the house

The parlour would have been gloomy, for the windows were small and the ceiling low; but the present proprietor had rendered it more cheerful, by opening one end into a small conservatory roofed with glass, and divided from the parlour by a partition of the same. I have never before seen this very pleasing manner of uniting the comforts of an apartment with the beauties of a garden.[22]

The technical innovations described above allowed a new type of conservatory with greater levels of light and more efficiently regulated heat, rendering it better equipped to house permanent displays of plants and flowers. Conservatories thus became more agreeable places in which to spend time, and so they began to be positioned nearer to the house. This desire to integrate the conservatory into the living accommodation was a natural outcome of the late 18th-century impulse to achieve a closer relationship between the house and its landscape. The main reception rooms were generally at first-floor level (the piano nobile) in grander Georgian houses but in the 19th century these began to be positioned on the ground floor, which enabled easier access to the gardens and facilitated the introduction of an integrated conservatory.

The appearance of full-height casements (known as French windows) in the 1780s or 1790s and the addition of balconies and verandas further allowed the landscape to be experienced from the interior, blurring the distinction between inside and outside. Flower gardens, terraces and balustrades were positioned around the house so that ornamental plants could constantly be seen and experienced, rather than being placed some distance away from the residence. As A W N Pugin (1812–52) and the architectural writer John Britton (1771–1857) observed in 1825, 'the principal floor is brought so near to the level of the lawn that ... its verdure and decorations have become almost a continuation of the furniture of the morning and drawing-rooms, and in summer vies with them in hourly occupation.'[23] Well-known contemporary examples of residences in which the interior is closely linked with the outside are The Deepdene and Knowle Cottage. The Deepdene at Dorking, Surrey, was a Palladian mansion built in the 1760s. It was acquired in 1808 by Thomas Hope, who remodelled it, adding a newly fashionable conservatory as well as pergolas, loggias and French windows. Knowle Cottage in Sidmouth, Devon, a cottage orné built *c* 1820, was designed with a conservatory in order to link the accommodation with the ornamental garden and the wider landscape beyond (Fig 11).

Repton was one of the key figures in encouraging this closer link between the house, garden and landscape, and throughout his career he produced many designs for conservatories and French windows.[24] Luscombe Castle in Devon, which he designed with John Nash (1752–1835) in 1800, is one of the earliest examples of the incorporation of a conservatory into the social space of the main house (Figs 12 and 13). It leads directly off the drawing room, which consequently has views of the park not only from its own windows but also through the glass walls of the conservatory. It is Gothic in style and was fitted with removable windows so that it could be used as a veranda in warm weather. In deciding on the position of the house, Nash had been inspired by

Fig 11

The picturesque Knowle Cottage
in Sidmouth, Devon. [Reproduced
by kind permission of the Syndics
of Cambridge University Library
(Rel.d.83.1)]

Sir Uvedale Price (1747–1829), author of *Essay on the Picturesque* (1794).
Price was an important influence on the emergence of the natural English
landscape garden and he encouraged garden designers to take inspiration from
landscape painters to achieve the Picturesque aesthetic. At Luscombe, Nash
accommodated the building to the scenery and designed specific rooms to have
certain views, resulting in an irregular plan that was well adapted to include a
conservatory in a way that could not be achieved so easily in the symmetrical
house plans favoured in the 18th century.

Repton, in fact, often preferred the conservatory to be detached from the
house and placed in the flower garden instead. He objected to its integration
on the basis of 'its want of conformity to the neighbouring mansion, since it is
difficult to make the glass roof of a conservatory architectural, whether Grecian
or Gothic.' Furthermore, he stated that 'such an appendage, however it may
increase its interior comfort, will never add to the external ornament of a house
of regular architecture.' He also objected to a conservatory being 'immediately
attached to a room constantly inhabited', because 'the smell and damp from
a large body of earth in the beds, or pots, is often more powerful than the
fragrance of the plants; therefore [it] should always be separated from the house,
by a lobby, or small anti-room.'[25] One of his favourite plans was to attach the
conservatory to the house via a flower passage.

Despite his objections, Repton acknowledged that 'among the refinements
of modern luxury may be reckoned that of attaching a green-house to some

Fig 12
Luscombe Castle in Devon, from
Humphry Repton's 'Red Book', in
which he presented 'before' and
'after' views to show his client.
[© Country Life 5501819]

Fig 13
The interior of the conservatory at
Luscombe Castle. [© Country Life
5501818]

room in the mansion, a fashion with which I have ... often been required to comply.'[26] As at Luscombe Castle, he frequently designed the conservatory to be accessed directly from the drawing room or one of the other principal living rooms. This is illustrated by a plan produced in *Fragments on the Theory and Practice of Landscape Gardening* (1816) in which the music room (6) opens into the orangery (4), which in turn leads to the conservatory (2) via the flower passage (3) (Fig 14). Repton also encouraged the addition of a conservatory to existing houses, notably when they had an irregular Gothic plan, as this

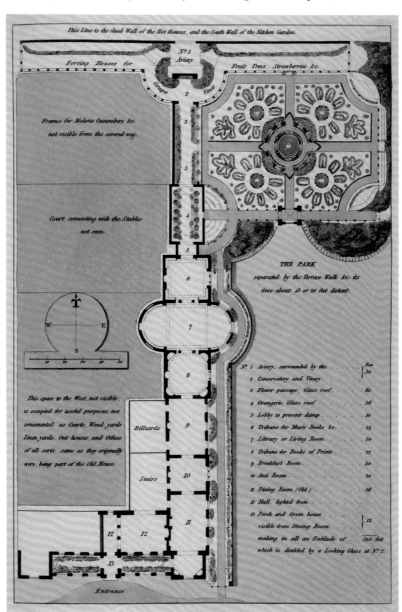

Fig 14

Repton's plan of a house in *Fragments on the Theory and Practice of Landscape Gardening* (1816). [Reproduced by kind permission of the Syndics of Cambridge University Library (Harley-Mason.a.50)]

especially lent itself to an asymmetrical extension. In *Observations on the Theory and Practice of Landscape Gardening* (1803) he included a plan indicating the potential position of a conservatory to show 'how conveniently the comforts of modern habitations may be adapted to ancient magnificence' (Fig 15).[27] At Harlestone House, Northamptonshire, an early 18th-century house thought to be the model for Jane Austen's Mansfield Park, Repton was employed (at some point before 1810) to carry out alterations to the house and grounds, which included the addition of a large conservatory.

Largely through Repton's influence, the conservatory thus became a key room in the Regency era.[28] It was described by Papworth in 1818 as:

> an embellishment of the most agreeable kind to the garden and also to the mansion; for instead of being, as originally, in a removed situation, the conservatory is now placed in connexion with the house itself, with which it elegantly combines, and gives an apartment highly valuable from its beauty and cheerfulness.[29]

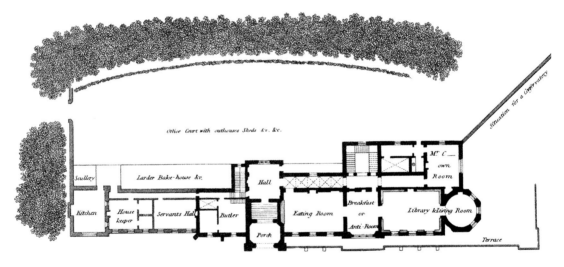

Fig 15

Repton's plan of a house in *Observations on the Theory and Practice of Landscape Gardening* (1803). [Source: Historic England Archive]

Some examples became particularly well known during the period, such as the conservatory at Sezincote House, Gloucestershire (1805–7), designed by Samuel Pepys Cockerell, Thomas Daniell and Repton (Fig 16). Built for Sir Charles Cockerell, who had spent time working for the East India Company, the house is in an exuberant Mogul style complete with a curving conservatory lit by full-height peacock-tail windows. Conservatories also began to make an appearance in contemporary literature as an indication of wealth and status. In Jane Austen's *Emma* (1815), Mr Weston complains of the rather grand and demanding Mrs Churchill, saying that she is 'too weak to get into her conservatory without having both his arm and his uncle's!'

With the improvements in glasshouse design, and Loudon's advocacy of the benefits of greenhouses and gardening generally, the desire for a conservatory began to filter down the social scale by the second decade of the 19th century. As Loudon observed, though neither the conservatory nor flower garden was essential to a suburban residence, 'they are yet additions which few persons, who

Fig 16
Sezincote House in
Gloucestershire (1805–7)
designed by Samuel Pepys
Cockerell, Thomas Daniell and
Repton. [© Julian Civiero]

can afford the expense will like to be without.'[30] Encouraged by the contemporary press, which was replete with horticultural journals and magazines, treatises on garden layouts and designs, and plans for greenhouses of all descriptions, the middle-class householder received plentiful advice about how to build and look after their conservatory. Loudon in particular provided garden and greenhouse plans for houses with a relatively small amount of land, such as those he included for villa grounds from one perch (25.2 sq m) to 100 acres (40.5ha) in *Hints on the Formation of Gardens and Pleasure Grounds* (1812).

Regrettably, very few of these early conservatories built by middle-class householders have survived, mainly due to the cost involved in their maintenance – an expense that usually only wealthier families could meet over succeeding generations. Contemporary publications such as those by Loudon, Papworth and Tod therefore provide an invaluable insight into the construction, design, layout and use of the more modest conservatories in the earlier part of the 19th century.

The appropriate location for conservatories

In large houses, few objects connected with them produce a more splendid effect, or contribute more to luxurious enjoyment during winter, than a large well kept conservatory.[31]

The new informality of social life

As conservatories were being increasingly added to existing houses and incorporated into new house plans, one of the key considerations was their most appropriate location. According to Loudon, in order for the conservatory to be truly enjoyed as a luxury, it was essential for it to be attached to the house, the most desirable location being next to the breakfast parlour or library, which was then the most important family sitting room (Fig 17). 'If', Loudon wrote, 'it communicates by spacious glass doors, and the parlour is judiciously furnished with mirrors, and bulbous flowers in water-glasses, the effect will be greatly heightened, and growth, verdure, gay colours, and fragrance, blended with books, sofas, and all the accompaniments of social and polished life.'[32] This type of arrangement was typical of the more informal manner of entertaining and socialising that had developed by the early 19th century. Instead of the rigid 18th-century conversation circle, social life in households was increasingly based on a more fluid arrangement in which family and guests conversed in groups, read books or walked amidst the plants in the conservatory. This change is aptly illustrated by Repton's illustrated poem in *Fragments on the Theory and Practice of Landscape Gardening* (1816):

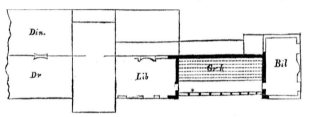

Fig 17

Plan of a house from Loudon's *The Green-House Companion* (1832).

[© Royal Botanic Gardens, Kew]

Fig 18

Plan of a house from Loudon's *The Green-House Companion* (1832).

[© Royal Botanic Gardens, Kew]

No more the cedar parlour's formal gloom
With dullness chills, 'tis now the living room,
Where guests to whim, to task or fancy true
Scatter'd in groups, their different plans pursue.
Here politicians eagerly relate
The last day's news, or the last night's debate.
Here books of poetry and books of prints
Furnish aspiring artists with new hints ...
Here, midst exotic plants, the curious maid
Of Greek and Latin seems no more afraid.

For Loudon, the second-best situation for the conservatory was therefore where it could communicate with the drawing room, the air of which would be perfumed by the scent of the plants (Fig 18). One of his proposals was for a drawing room projecting from the house in the form of a pentagon or an octagon and enclosed by a conservatory on all sides except for that on which it is entered from the house. The flower passage that Repton had favoured was also a possibility, but it would have to open directly into, and be visible from, one of the reception rooms.

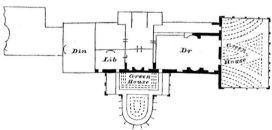

The conservatory thus became an integral part of the physical and social space of late Georgian households. At Shrubland Park, Suffolk (1770–72), following the remodelling by J P Gandy-Deering from 1831 to 1833, the new conservatory opened into the boudoir and became the main living space in the house for a greater part of the year (Fig 19). In *Illustrations of the Public Buildings of London* (1825), Britton and Pugin observed how the drawing room, library, music room, conservatory and billiard room were now disposed en suite, when they had previously been separated according to male or female occupation. By means of large folding doors, the reception rooms could form one large apartment, 'embracing all the objects of study and amusement they individually possess', and putting an end to the gender segregation that dictated some aspects of social life.[33] This arrangement is illustrated at St Dunstan's Lodge (1825), one of the villas designed by Decimus Burton in Regent's Park, which has an enfilade consisting of three rooms on the garden front, with two large rooms for parties on one end and a circular conservatory on the other.

Fig 19
The conservatory at Shrubland Park, Suffolk, added by J P Gandy-Deering in 1831–3. [© Historic England Archive BB99/06188]

The most advantageous positions for the conservatory

Contemporary gardeners and architects mostly agreed that the conservatory should be situated as close to the house as possible, although there was some difference of opinion. Charles McIntosh, in *The Greenhouse, Hot House and Stove* (1838), stated that 'the most proper situation for the conservatory is either in the flower-garden, where it should be a detached structure, or adjoining to the mansion, of which it may be said to form a part'.[34] In *The Exotic Gardener* (1814) John Cushing acknowledged the difficulty in giving advice about precise locations because

> The various differing ideas in planning, and building these edifices; every one suiting his convenience and situation, renders it almost impracticable to say which is the best; however, when a house for this purpose ... is intended to be built, the greatest attention should be paid to the choice of situation; preferring a dry, airy, but sheltered and warm aspect.[35]

Despite the individual requirements in each case, it was thought that the best position for a conservatory was on the south side of the house, preferably to the SSE, from where it would receive the most sunlight. This corresponded to the usual position of the breakfast room, which thereby benefited from the morning sun and enticed the occupants to venture into the garden. It was also preferable for the plants, explained Loudon, as the morning sun 'dries up the damps generated during the night' and illuminates 'their foliage and flowers to the spectators in the living-room'. A conservatory with a west or even south-west aspect was not advisable because it required much more fuel to keep it heated.[36]

In *A Treatise on Forming, Improving, and Managing Country Residences* (1806) Loudon provided the plan for a house with a large conservatory and vinery he had designed for a 'small place in the neighbourhood of London, where no prospect, or good external views, can be obtained from the windows' (Fig 20). The conservatory was thus positioned to be accessed via the three principal living rooms: the library, drawing room and dining room, from which 'agreeable perspectives through the conservatory may be obtained, even while sitting at table'. Furthermore, all the bedrooms on the south side of the house had windows coming down to the floor and looking entirely into the conservatory. The conservatory was by these means completely integrated into the plan of the house, providing a room for entertainment as well as making up for the absence of views. Loudon expressed the hope that as 'a conservatory is one of the greatest luxuries both to a principal residence in the country, and a small villa or cottage near the town, perhaps it [the plan] may tend to promote their more general introduction'.[37]

William Cobbett, in *The English Gardener* (1829), also argued that in order for a conservatory to be 'an agreeable thing' it should be very near the house. He saw it as a means of giving pleasure, 'for the rational amusement and occupation, of persons who would otherwise be employed in things irrational; if not mischievous'. If it were at a distance from the house, the inhabitants would invariably not make the journey to it in cold, wet weather, thereby precluding its beneficial effects. In Cobbett's view, it should therefore be erected next to the house, preferably on the south side, 'and a door into it, and a window, or windows looking into it, from any room of the house in which people frequently sit, makes the thing extremely beautiful and agreeable.'[38] Loudon concurred,

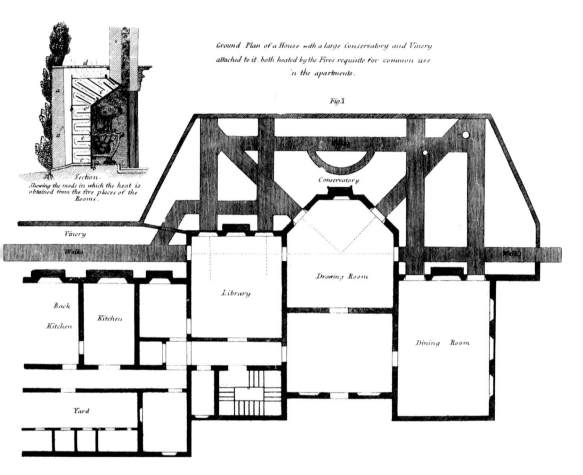

Ground Plan of a House with a large Conservatory and Vinery
attached to it, both heated by the Fires requisite for common use
in the apartments.

Fig.I

Section.
Showing the mode in which the heat is
obtained from the fire places of the
Rooms.

Vinery

Walk

Conservatory

Drawing Room

Library

Back
Kitchen

Kitchen

Dining Room

Yard

Fig 20

Plan of a house from Loudon's
*A Treatise on Forming, Improving,
and Managing Country Residences*
(1806). [Source: Historic England
Archive]

claiming that 'a green-house, however excellent and well managed, if it cannot be seen and entered without going into the open air, can never afford half its appropriate enjoyments during the winter season.'[39]

Papworth was more particular than Cobbett in his recommendations. He proposed that the conservatory should adjoin the breakfast room or morning sitting room, because of 'the cheerfulness and health which plants afford at that time', and never the drawing or dining rooms, because 'plants absorb in the evening a large portion of that quality of vital air that is essential to human existence.'[40] Despite this assertion, in a number of the plans he presented in *Rural Residences* (1818) the conservatory does in fact open out into the drawing room. In Plate X, which depicts a farmhouse or ornamental cottage, the drawing room is next to the conservatory (Fig 21). Similarly, in Plate XV, which shows a villa, designed as a residence for a small family, the drawing room leads on to the music room, which opens straight into the conservatory (Fig 22). In some of the larger late Georgian houses, the conservatory was strategically placed to mask the extensive servants' quarters, as at Dodington Park in Gloucestershire (1797–c 1817) where James Wyatt (1746–1813) designed a quadrant conservatory extending from the library to conceal the service wing.

Fig 21
One of John Papworth's designs
for a cottage orné in *Rural
Residences* (1818). [Source:
Historic England Archive]

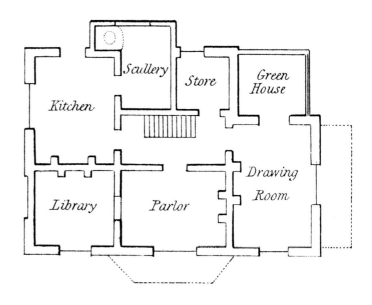

Fig 22
One of Papworth's designs for a
villa in *Rural Residences* (1818).
[Source: Historic England
Archive]

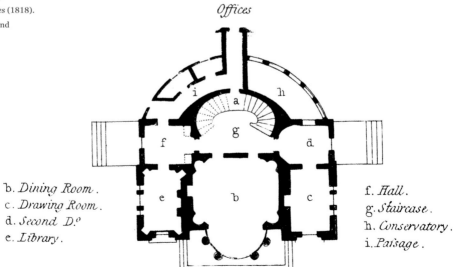

Offices

b. *Dining Room.*
c. *Drawing Room.*
d. *Second D.º*
e. *Library.*

f. *Hall.*
g. *Staircase.*
h. *Conservatory.*
i. *Passage.*

Many published plans for suburban or country residences invariably had gardens surrounding the house and could thus incorporate a conservatory in the optimum location. The most suitable suburban residences for having a conservatory, Loudon observed, were those that were either detached or in pairs. If the house was small, the usual way of attaching a greenhouse or conservatory was by placing it against the gable end.[41] In London, where gardens were smaller and more likely to adjoin only the rear of the property, greenhouses were sometimes placed behind the house on the tops of kitchens and other offices.[42] As the architect and Professor of Perspective Richard Brown described in his late work *Domestic Architecture* (1841), just as in the country, where conservatories were built on the ground floor next to the drawing room or breakfast room, so in London, where the drawing room was often on the first floor, they were placed on this level as well.[43] A fascinating example of this is the conservatory constructed by Tod for George Farrant in Upper Brook Street, London (1812), which is situated 11ft (3.4m) above the surface of the yard behind the dwelling so that the floor is on the same level as the drawing room with which it communicates (Fig 23).

The conservatory was thus, wherever possible, adjoined to the living rooms of the house, especially the drawing room. Cushing wrote that 'for conservatories in particular ... if attached or contiguous to the drawing room, the more pleasant; as they thereby afford an agreeable retreat at seasons, when other parts of the garden cannot be visited without considerable inconvenience.'[44] The publications of the period are full of plans in which this arrangement is found, mostly for ground-floor conservatories. Charles Middleton, in *The Architect and Builder's Miscellany, or Pocket Library; Containing Original Picturesque Designs in Architecture* (1812), provided a plan and elevation for a Palladian-inspired house in which one of the pavilions contains a conservatory opening into both the drawing room and the music room (Figs 24 and 25). In the majority of the plans included in Tod's *Plans, Elevations and Sections* (1812), the drawing room opens into the conservatory through French windows. The two conservatories executed for John Jackson at North

Fig 23

A greenhouse constructed for George Farrant in Upper Brook Street, London, by George Tod. [© Royal Botanic Gardens, Kew]

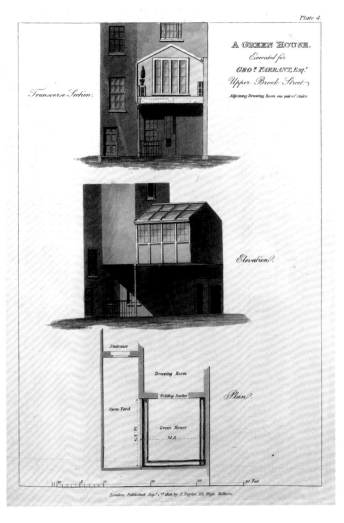

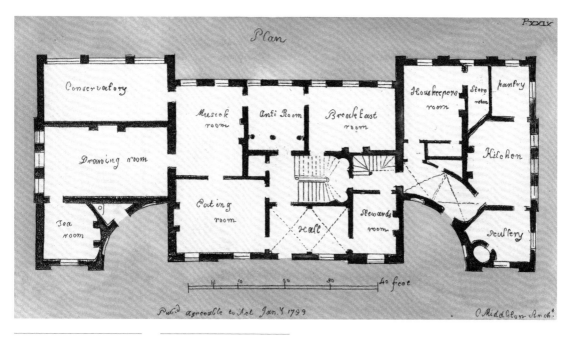

Fig 24 (above)
One of Charles Middleton's plans
for a house in *The Architect and
Builder's Miscellany* (1812).
[© The British Library Board
(1489.g.60, Plate XXIX)]

Fig 25 (below)
The elevation of this design
in *The Architect and Builder's
Miscellany* (1812).
[© The British Library Board
(1489.g.60, Plate XXX)]

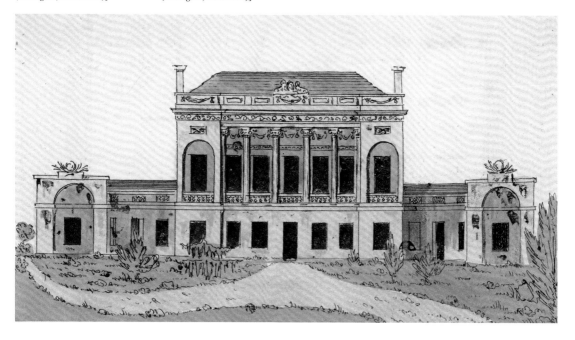

End, Hammersmith, for example, adjoin the drawing room, with which they communicate by glazed folding doors (Fig 26). In *Hints on the Formation of Gardens*, Loudon's plan for a villa with 3–6 acres (1.2–2.4ha) for a family of six to eight persons (Fig 27) has a veranda (c) adjacent to the dining room (d), which opens into a substantial conservatory (f). Loudon advised that in large houses the conservatory should be separated from the drawing room by glass doors or windows opening down to the floor, 'so as to give the idea of the drawing room and conservatory forming but one room.'[45]

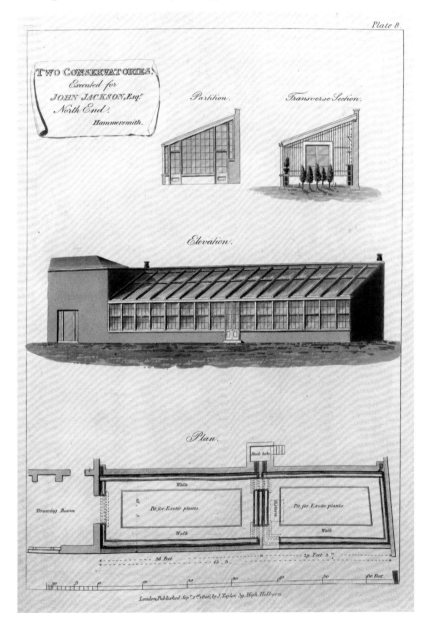

Fig 26

Two conservatories executed for John Jackson at North End, Hammersmith, by George Tod, in *Plans, Elevations and Sections* (1812). [© Royal Botanic Gardens, Kew]

Fig 27

Loudon's plan for a villa with 3–6

acres (1.2–2.4ha) for a family of

six to eight persons, in *Hints on*

the Formation of Gardens (1812).

[© The British Library Board

(441.g.21, Plate 6, Fig 1)]

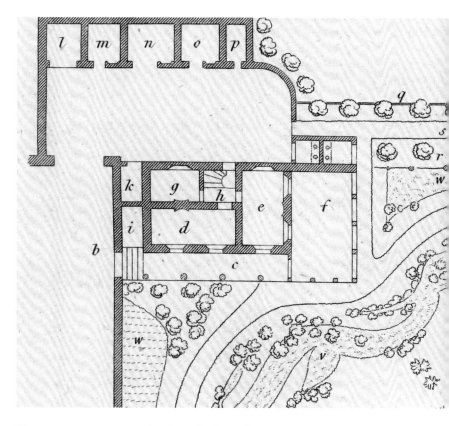

The conservatory as the female domain

In the early 19th-century house, certain rooms had gender associations: the library and study were traditionally seen as the male domain, while the drawing room was the natural environment of the ladies. As Jill Franklin mentions, a man would refer to 'his wife's drawing room'.[46] The typical attachment of the conservatory to the drawing room therefore brought the conservatory within the female domain and it became particularly associated with women. An article in *The Gardener's Magazine* (April 1826) about a conservatory recently added to The Grange, Hampshire, noted that 'into this spacious area of perpetual spring, are directed the windows of those apartments dedicated to the ladies.'[47] The connection between the conservatory and the female inhabitants of the house also developed from the idea, encouraged by Loudon, that 'women were "naturally" indoor people and men outdoor.'[48] In *The Green-House Companion*, Loudon remarked that 'a green-house is in a peculiar degree the care of the female part of the family, and forms an interesting scene of recreation to a mother and her daughters, at a season of the year when there is but little inducement to walk in the kitchen-garden, and nothing to do in the parterre or the shrubbery.'[49] At Wrest Park in Bedfordshire (1834–9), designed by the owner Thomas Philip, 2nd Earl de Grey, the conservatory opens directly out of the countess's sitting room, the doors of which are aligned so that she could see the Italian garden through the conservatory and to the kitchen garden beyond (Figs 28 and 29).

Fig 28
The conservatory at Wrest
Park, Bedfordshire. [© Historic
England Archive DP029995]

Fig 29

The countess's sitting room at
Wrest Park opens directly into the
conservatory. [© Historic England
Archive DP087693]

The conservatory, furthermore, was used primarily to display flowers, and women were regarded as having by nature an inherently stronger response to, and love of, flowers than men. This association had been well established before the 19th century. In 1778 Mrs Philip Lybbe Powys (1756–1808) remarked after her visit to Middleton Park, Oxfordshire that, 'as her ladyship is, according to the fashion, a botanist, she has a pretty flower garden going out of the library.'[50] Dr Lindley, a professor of botany at the University of London, published *Ladies' Botany; or, A Familiar Introduction to the Study of the Natural System of Botany* in 1834, partly because he was 'anxious that the endless variety of beautiful objects which the Vegetable world so prodigally strews before our path should, with those who from their habits of life and gentler feelings are the most sensible to the charms of nature, become something beyond a vague sentiment of undefined admiration'.[51] Lindley's *Ladies' Botany* was one of many books published specifically to instruct women in the art of gardening and the study of botany, a market that was dominated by Jane Loudon. In *Instructions in Gardening for Ladies* (1840) she affirmed that 'whatever doubts may be entertained as to the practicability of a lady attending to the culture of culinary vegetables and fruit-trees, none can exist respecting her management of the flower-garden, as that is pre-eminently a woman's department.' The reason she gave for this, however, is nothing to do with the supposed notion of women's superior sensitivity to nature, but because 'the culture of flowers implies the lightest possible kind of garden labour.'[52]

Design

The defective construction of Hothouses, both in respect to the beauty of their form and the admission of light, has long been acknowledged; the former by men of taste, and the latter by enlightened horticulturalists. ... In proportion as they are dignified by architectural forms, in the same ratio will the plants to be inclosed [sic] suffer from the want of the light excluded by the masonry.[53]

'Architectural' versus 'not architectural'

While the most suitable location of the conservatory within the house was widely agreed upon, the question of its stylistic integration also had to be addressed, whether it was designed as an integral part of a new house or attached to an existing one. Prior to the invention of the curved iron glazing bar in 1816, the roofs of greenhouses and conservatories invariably took the form of what Loudon termed 'lean-to shed-looking glass roofs'. He regarded such structures as fit only to be positioned in the kitchen garden and unsuitable for conservatories which, as they provided 'the gaiety and beauty of spring and summer amidst the frigid scenes of winter', should be appended to the house. He acknowledged the attempt to render conservatories more stylistically pleasing by disguising their 'shed-like appearance' with stone piers and parapet walls but found that this invariably led to loss of light to the detriment of the plants.[54] A distinction thus arose between what Loudon termed 'architectural' and 'not architectural' conservatories'.[55]

The discrepancy between what was suitable from a horticultural perspective and what was architecturally desirable was not easily resolved. The curvilinear iron-framed structures advocated by Loudon in 1818 were not generally regarded, certainly at this early stage, as aesthetically compatible with masonry structures. There are some examples of curvilinear conservatories attached to houses, such as Burton's small structure on the gable end of The Holme, and the early 19th-century half-domed conservatory on the front of Brooklands in Sawston, Cambridgeshire, but they are more often found as detached structures in gardens (Fig 30). Loudon was therefore considerably advanced in asking,

Fig 30
The early 19th-century half-domed conservatory on the front of Brooklands in Sawston, Cambridgeshire. [Melissa Thompson]

'will not this substitution of new forms and almost perfect transparence be an improvement, gratifying both to the man of taste and the horticulturalist?' He believed that an edifice cannot be 'in correct taste, whose architecture is at variance with its use, which as it is rendered more beautiful, becomes less useful'.[56]

Papworth, for one, disagreed about the aesthetic merits of the 'new forms' of conservatories. He believed that

> Great judgement is required to connect it with the building so as to display its proposed forms without injury to those of the mansion itself; from which, indeed, it ought to receive its character, and of which it should assume to be a part; for, however agreeable variety may be, incongruity is always fatal to its charms with every well cultivated and tasteful mind.[57]

He did allow that 'habit perhaps has lessened the ill impression which a conservatory makes upon us when formed without reference to the edifice to which it is attached.'[58] His own designs, though, always derived their character from the house, as is illustrated by Plate XXI, which depicts a Gothic conservatory suited to 'buildings of the same or of the castle character' (Fig 31).[59] Although Burton initially showed interest in the curvilinear form, he too came to favour architectural conservatories that combined an elegant masonry structure supporting large window openings with wood- or iron-framed glass roofs.

The conservatory designed by C R Cockerell for The Grange in Hampshire in 1824 was regarded as a perfect compromise by Charles McIntosh in *The Greenhouse, Hot House and Stove* (1838). 'This house', he declared, 'in regard to architectural and horticultural proportions, two important points in similar structures, but seldom agreeing together ... is, in our opinion, the most complete thing of the kind that we have seen, either in this country or the continent.' The large conservatory is treated architecturally in the employment of slender pilasters to divide the bays and in the highly ornamented mouldings on the internal cast-iron columns, while also being horticultural in its expanse of glazing on the elevations and M-shaped glazed roof which, as McIntosh points out, 'might be continued to any extent'.[60]

Fig 31

Papworth's plan and elevation for a Gothic conservatory in *Rural Residences* (1818). [Source: Historic England Archive]

Conservatories in harmony with the house

Loudon initially advocated curvilinear conservatories in all situations but later conceded that a conservatory should harmonise with the house to which it is attached, although he insisted that 'much less will affect this harmony than what is generally imagined. Few old villas, on a small or moderate scale, display much of design in their masonry or brick work. With all such, any plain form of glazed structure will accord'[61] (Fig 32). He thought the architectural unity of the house and conservatory was to come about not by assimilation but by a consciously composed difference.[62] Despite Loudon's assertions and the widely accepted superiority of the curvilinear shape, conservatories continued to be built with lean-to or pitched glass roofs in a style which imitated that of the house. Loudon himself presented such designs, perhaps realising that he was fighting a losing battle, at least as far as the design of adjoining conservatories was concerned. In *The Green-House Companion* (1832) he acknowledged that in houses embellished with architectural furnishings such as columns, pediments and cornices, then such details should influence the style of the conservatory, but never in a way that interferes with the light, heating or ventilation.

Fig 32

The elevation of a villa by Loudon in *The Green-House Companion* (1832). [© Royal Botanic Gardens, Kew]

Architectural eclecticism

Late 18th- and early 19th-century architecture was distinguished by an exuberant variety of historical styles which were duly applied to conservatories with equal fervour. As Loudon pointed out:

> Where a house is characterised by some particular style of architecture, it is easy to impress that style on the green-house. The form of the heads of the doors and windows, peculiar to the different orders of Gothic architecture, can readily be imitated in the front sashes and doors of a green-house; and in the case of Grecian architecture, the mouldings of any orders are readily applied to the styles, rails, and bars, and to the standards and other posts: and even columns may be introduced in very considerable erections.[63]

Papworth presents numerous styles for villas with attached conservatories, from Gothic to Classical, and Brown's plans and elevations in *Domestic Architecture* (1841) also perfectly encapsulate the freedom with which architects plundered the past to offer their clients all manner of dwellings. It was possible to live in a Tudor mansion house based on the period of Henry VIII with a conservatory embellished with a continuous drip mould over the tall glazed openings, or a villa in the Florentine style with a conservatory in the form of a pavilion with a pedimented tripartite window and moulded apron (Fig 33). What is notable about Brown's collection of designs is how conservatories, by this time, are incorporated into the living space as a matter of course.

One of the most striking conservatories in the Tudor style is that at Mamhead House in Devon, designed by Anthony Salvin in 1827–33. The house has an asymmetrical plan with a south-west service wing that continues as a four-bay, cloister-like conservatory with moulded Tudor-arched doorways. These have glazed doors with iron tracery, the verticals cast to look like slender buttresses with offsets. The spandrels have naturalistic flower carving and the parapet is carved with a quotation in Gothic script from Chaucer's *Roman de la Rose* (Fig 34). Another exuberant conservatory in the Tudor style is at Orton Hall, Peterborough, which was extensively rebuilt in 1835 to the design of H Smith of London. It has a pierced crenelated parapet and the bays are divided

Fig 33
Richard Brown's design for a
Florentine Villa in *Domestic
Architecture* (1841).
[© The British Library Board
(1265.f.21, Plate XVIII)]

Fig 34
The gothic conservatory at
Mamhead House in Devon.
[© Sarah Clarke https://
www.flickr.com/photos/
tworedboots/2541766053/
in/photostream/]

by buttresses surmounted by tall finials. The six Tudor-arched windows are crisscrossed with bands of coloured glass bearing the family motto 'Let Curzon hold what Curzon held'. The interior is no less elaborate with its hammer-beam roof, which has crenelated collar beams, elaborate pendants at the bottom end of the hammer posts and arched tie beams resting on corbels in the forms of gargoyles (Figs 35 and 36). It must have been such conservatories as these that inspired Pugin's derisive description:

> On one side of the house machicolated parapets, embrasures, bastions and all the show of strong defence; and round the corner of the building a conservatory leading to the principal rooms through which a whole company of horsemen might penetrate at one smash into the very heart of the mansion! For who would hammer against nailed portals when he could kick his way through the greenhouse?[64]

Houses in the classical style could equally well accommodate a conservatory. In the early 1820s William Atkinson designed one in the style of a Greek temple at The Deepdene in Surrey, and Gandy-Deering's design at Shrubland Park is in the Italianate style, complete with balustraded parapet. Palladian villas also provided inspiration for architects such as James Wyatt, who used the form of the wing terminating in a pavilion for the quadrant conservatory at Dodington Park in Gloucestershire. Similarly, Joseph Bonomi incorporated a curved conservatory at Eastwell Park in Kent (1794).

Fig 35 (below)
The Tudoresque conservatory at Orton Hall in Peterborough.
[Melissa Thompson]

Fig 36 (below right)
The no-less exuberant interior of the conservatory at Orton Hall.
[Melissa Thompson]

Advice and manufacturers

In addition to providing designs of conservatories, contemporary publications offered advice on how to build them. In *Remarks on the Construction of Hothouses* (1817) Loudon stated that as architects had not until very lately deemed the design of conservatories of sufficient importance to master new improvements, it was 'scientific gardeners' who were 'certainly the best judges, and ought to be the best designers of hothouses'.[65] The improvements in greenhouse design were due, he claimed, to the fact that 'mansion architects' were no longer in sole charge of their design.[66] In *The Green-House Companion* he still advised those who wished to erect a conservatory to consult an architect to ensure it accorded with the house, but then to consult a gardener to establish the best position, and lastly a manufacturer of glasshouses to provide a plan and estimate. In order to spare expense, Loudon suggested that the former two services could be dispensed with if the prospective owner had well considered the options himself.[67] An example of this is the villa in Shepherd's Bush belonging to T S Barber, which Loudon referred to as having been 'most tastefully and economically arranged, from the proprietor's own designs'.[68]

Specialist manufacturers

The prospective owners of conservatories were advised to build the structure in early summer so that it had time to settle before the plants were arranged.[69] The principles of construction were in all respects the same as for greenhouses except that a pit or bed of earth was dug in a conservatory.[70] They were built by the growing number of specialist manufacturers who advertised in the pages of the horticultural press or were recommended in other publications. In his preface to *Plans, Elevations and Sections* (1812) George Tod refers to himself as a 'Surveyor and Hot-House Builder' and he only includes examples that have been executed from his own designs and those of W T Aiton, His Majesty's Gardener at Kew and Kensington. Loudon's preferred manufacturers were Messrs W and D Bailey of High Holborn, whom he recommended in *The Green-House Companion* among other publications. Mrs Loudon mentioned in *The Ladies' Companion to the Flower-Garden* (1842) that 'very excellent and ornamental greenhouses in iron are constructed by Messrs Cottam and Hallan, and wooden houses may be made by any carpenter or joiner.'[71] An issue of *The Gardener's Magazine* in October 1826 contained advertisements for John Lang, Hothouse Builder, who manufactured and erected greenhouses in any part of the country; and J W Thompson, who provided plans and estimates for erecting and heating all horticultural buildings.[72]

Some manufacturers were proactive in publicising their successful commissions. Jones and Clark (established in 1818 by Thomas Clark, an early prefabricator and builder of metal glasshouses) sent to *The Gardeners' Magazine* in January 1827 an engraved perspective and description of the conservatory at The Grange, Hampshire, which they erected in 1824 for Alexander Baring MP. They explain how the whole of the conservatory, with the exception of the brickwork and stonework, was executed at their 'manufactory' in Lionel Street, Birmingham, and afterwards erected in its present situation by their own workmen. The letter ends with the mention of two further examples of their work commissioned by high-profile clients.

Rebuilding, reuse and adaptation

In some cases, conservatories were rebuilt or reused. In *The Green-House Companion* Loudon mentioned that in the neighbourhood of large towns, old or used greenhouses were frequently put up for sale at low rates. He warned against buying these, however, especially if the conservatory was to be attached to a house, as 'there is not one green-house in a hundred that will fit two different situations.'[73] Despite this, the practice continued at both ends of the scale. The detached conservatory at Bretton Hall in Yorkshire (1827), one of Bailey's most celebrated structures, was dismantled after the death of Mrs Beamont in 1832 and sold at auction. It fetched £560, a fraction of the £14,000 it had cost to erect. The cost for the ironwork alone was between £3,000 and £4,000, a reflection of the amount needed as well as the intricacy of the design. When the ironwork was put up it was said to have swayed about in the wind, but as soon as the glass was put in, the structure became firm and strong.

As the design of conservatories evolved, existing examples were sometimes altered according to new improvements. At the villa in Roehampton belonging to W Gosling, Tod made alterations to the conservatory which adjoined the drawing room in 1812 (*see* Fig 22). He explained that it was originally constructed with a slate roof 'which is found to be injurious to the growth of plants' and so he substituted it with a glass roof. He altered the flue, made the conservatory wider, and also introduced improvements in its layout by constructing an aviary in one corner and a fountain in the middle with an arbour and seat immediately behind, against the back wall. Finally, 'a transverse screen of treillage work' was added under each alternate rafter and on the back wall for the purpose of training creeping or running plants. 'The whole is finished', Tod claimed, 'in a manner superior to most buildings of this description.'[74]

Environmental conditions

[A conservatory] is entirely a work of art: the plants inclosed [sic] are in the most artificial situation in which they can be placed, and require constant and unremitting attention to counteract the tendency of that artificial situation to destroy them. [They] are not only in an artificial and injurious state as to the soil, but also as to their climate, and especially as to heat, light, and air.[75]

Ventilation
Plants kept in the artificial environment of conservatories needed to be well ventilated in order to thrive. Conservatories were therefore constructed so that the window sashes could be opened or removed, leaving the plants in the open air and exposed to the weather. The usual method was for the walls and roof to have sashes which slid in grooves and could be let down or drawn up as required, while the doors at the ends could be left open to let in air. Some conservatories were designed to allow the complete removal of certain sections of glass, such as Papworth's plan for a Gothic conservatory in which the glass of the centre part is intended to be removed during certain seasons of the year. Other designs allowed for the complete removal of the roof so that the plants could be exposed to the open air in summer.

In conservatories with fixed roofs and in curvilinear structures it was usual to have opening sashes in front and opaque shutters at the top of the rear wall to allow a current to circulate inside. In *An Encyclopaedia of Gardening* (1835) Loudon provided an illustration of the ventilation system for what he termed a polyprosopic conservatory, which resembled a curvilinear one except that the surface was over a number of faces (Fig 37). The faces were hinged at their upper angles and rods were connected at the lower outside corners, terminating in chains which ran over pulleys in the top or above the back wall. By these means the whole roof could be opened, like Venetian blinds, either to allow each face or sash to catch the sun's rays or to admit a shower of rain. The plants could therefore at any time be subject to the same light, air, wind and dew as outside.

On occasion, plants also needed defending from the heat of the sun. Mackenzie's proposal for providing shade in a curvilinear conservatory was to place two external moveable ribs on a pivot at the top and to fasten canvas which could be stretched over the glass.[76]

Heating

The interior arrangement of conservatories was sometimes influenced by their proximity to the fireplaces in the adjacent rooms. This is illustrated by one of Loudon's plans for laying out a small plot of ground from a perch (25.2 sq m) to an acre (0.4ha). The conservatory, which forms a central and elaborate feature, consists of a long range with both ends (g) extending at right angles and curving round to meet in a central porch (*see* Fig 25; Fig 38). The main section opens into the four living rooms – the library (f), billiard room (e), dining room (c) and drawing room (d) – thus being entirely interwoven with all of the principal social spaces of the house. Loudon proposes that the most delicate plants are placed opposite the dining room and billiard room, so that the fires in these rooms heat that part of the conservatory to a sufficient temperature.[77] In *A Treatise on Forming, Improving, and Managing Country Residences* (1806) he provides a diagram and explanation showing the manner in which the heat is obtained from a fireplace in an adjacent room:

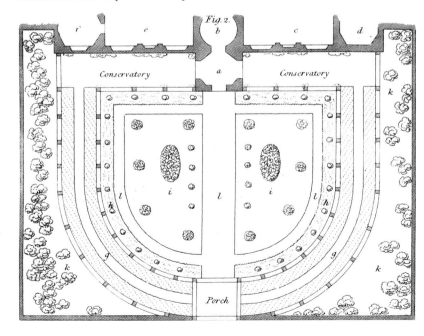

aa is a wall of masonry; bb two carron plates; ccc the passage for the air; which by being thus confined easily becomes heated, and passed out by the holes in the board d, which serve to diverge it regularly, and prevent any plants from being scorched by it. By pouring water upon the plate e, abundance of steam may be produced, when requisite.[78]

Fireplaces in adjoining rooms could not always provide sufficient heat for the conservatory. Before the method of heating through hot water pipes was perfected, Loudon suggested in 1812 that the best mode of constructing flues was to make a smoke chamber out of cast iron and surrounding it with brickwork. The iron conducted the heat, while the bricks absorbed it and gave it out slowly into the atmosphere of the conservatory. As this was expensive, however, he suggested that in ordinary cases the 'usual mode by brick sides and tyle [sic] covers is preferable'.[79] In the same year George Tod noted that an important improvement in the construction of flues was to form a void space underneath them, as it prevented the damp which rose from the ground obstructing the draught. He also recommended having a narrow space or cavity between the flue and wall, otherwise a great quantity of the heat in the flue would be absorbed by the wall (see Fig 26).[80] Experiments in steam heating were taking place during this period, with Papworth referring in 1818 to 'ingenious stoves and apparatus' that had lately been invented 'for the purposes of heating conservatories and greenhouses by steam'.[81] Water was heated and condensed in boilers and then sent through pipes which had been perforated to allow steam to escape into the conservatory. By 1825 R S Mickleham, a civil engineer, wrote that 'it is now generally admitted that steam is the most economical agent' and the most advantageous in its 'uniformity and certainty of regulating the temperature ... and from it not being liable to affect the chemical properties of the air, and thus injuring vegetable life'.[82]

Despite the advances in heating technology, it still required work on the part of the owner or their gardener to regulate the temperature inside conservatories. In 1818 Mr Kewley invented an 'Artificial Gardener', which he described as a simple self-regulating apparatus that carried out this work without any manual labour. The special thermometer or 'first-moving power', as he called it, would be set to the correct temperature, and as soon as the temperature in the conservatory exceeded this, the apparatus would begin to close the damper which admitted air to the fire until it was almost extinguished. If the temperature was still too high, the apparatus would open the windows until the necessary and exact climate was produced. They remained stationary until the temperature began to fall or rise. If the former, then the windows would first be closed and then the damper opened to admit air to the fire.[83]

Watering

The owners of conservatories were advised to water the plants either late in the evening or very early in the morning when the family was not present. There were several methods of watering the beds or pits. Loudon recommended that on the bottom these should be paved, on top of which should be placed a stratum of gravel six inches (152mm) deep, three inches (76mm) of green moss, followed by the soil. The plants could then easily be watered by pouring water into a tube placed in the stratum. To prevent plants requiring less moisture becoming waterlogged, they could be placed in a porous and non-retentive soil.[84] The plants would still need to be watered on the surface, so a syringe was recommended which would also refresh and cleanse the foliage and branches. For a wider distribution of water, owners and gardeners used small portable water engines. The engine was placed in a pail and discharged its stream of water, from a powerful current to a gentle dewfall (Fig 39). If vapour was required, it was created by pouring water onto a heated steam tube.

Perhaps the most intriguing method of watering was the 'artificial rain' invented around 1828 by Messrs Loddiges. It consisted of perforated lead pipes that were conducted horizontally under the glass roof and through which water could be passed in order to recreate a shower of rain. Loudon mentioned that it had been used successfully for 10 years in a magnificent palm house in Hackney. He did express concern, however, about the 'close damp effluvia from the earth, water, and plants of the conservatory' being 'disagreeable and unwholesome to human beings', and therefore recommended that the conservatory should be thoroughly ventilated before the family were expected to walk in it.[85]

Cockerell's design for the conservatory at The Grange (1824) incorporated hollow cast-iron columns which carried off the rainwater from the roof into drains and from thence into a large underground reservoir. This supplied all the water required for the conservatory, as well as for use in the event of fire, with the remainder being emptied beyond the house (Fig 40).

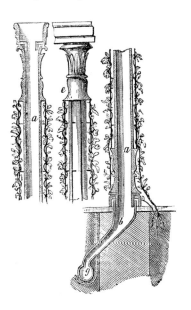

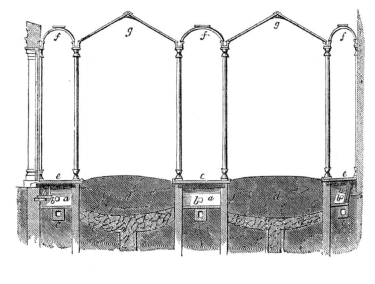

Interiors

Layout

As conservatories were now regarded as having a social function, much thought was given to their internal treatment to render them as attractive and engaging as possible. In terms of decoration, Cushing insisted that they should

> always be finished off in a tasteful manner, suitable to the purpose, and a good provision made for the various climbing plants, of which there are a considerable variety that constitute a principal share in ornamenting these departments, by being trained on the piers, or wires, hanging in fanciful festoonery along the roof of the house.[86]

He encouraged the practice of placing pots or urns in every part of the conservatory, on shelves or benches that may be over the flues and on any window stools. These, he asserted, 'if judiciously filled, with handsome growing and flowering plants, will add very materially in elegance to the contour of the whole group'[87] (Fig 41). Stands were erected to display plants to the best advantage, and in some instances, stages were made to revolve in order to present them in their varying aspects. Paths and walkways were laid out around the planted beds, sometimes paved in tiles or stone with iron grilles

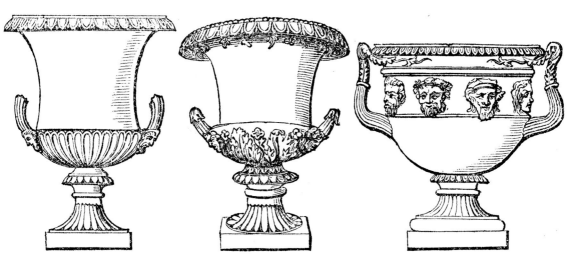

Fig 41

Examples of pots and urns suggested by Charles McIntosh in *The Greenhouse, Hot House, and Stove* (1838). [Reproduced by kind permission of the Syndics of University of Cambridge Library (B.17.32, p.241)]

to admit the heated air, or otherwise covered with gravel or turf. If the latter, it was advised that they should be kept smooth and firm through frequent rolling, and kept dry by the positioning of the flues and hot-water pipes directly underneath. The overall effect of such careful arrangements can be seen in the enjoyment of the occupants in the conservatory at The Grange, Hampshire (1824), illustrated in the *Gardeners' Magazine* (1827) (Fig 42).

A succinct and illuminating picture of the layout, building materials and practical workings of a Regency conservatory is provided by Tod, who described the structure he designed and built in 1812 for George Farrant in Upper Brook Street, London:

The floor is formed of strong timbers, on which are laid rough boarding,
and on the boarding are laid foot tile paving, bedded in Roman cement,
to prevent water from filtering through, when watering the plants. It has
a span roof of glass; one side is formed with sashes hung with weights,
to slide down; and the other side is brick-work, which terminates the
adjoining premises. The furnace is placed underneath, and the flue
ascends perpendicularly till it reaches the green-house, when it continues
round above the floor, and returns upon itself on that side which is brickwork, to a chimney placed at the north-east corner to discharge smoke.
There are fancy stages placed within; and the whole has a novel and
pleasant appearance from the drawing-room, particularly in the evening
when lighted with lamps.[88]

Another typical layout shown in Tod's designs is the conservatory for W
Linwood at Hackney, which is formed of two sections: the greenhouse, which
has a central stage for displaying plants surrounded by a walk; and the exotic
house, which is occupied by a pit for plunging plants and is also surrounded
by a walk (Fig 43). It was lit by lights on the roof hung by weights placed in
apertures in the back wall. The conservatory built by Tod for Richard Dickinson
in Hendon has a different layout with a central walk and stands positioned
along either wall (Fig 44).

A more elaborate internal treatment often included arbours with seats,
aviaries, fountains and fishponds, as at Belton House (Fig 45). Repton's
plan for the conservatory at Harewood House has a central section with two
large beds and flowering shrubs, with an apsidal projection for water or a
fountain. A description of the Gothic style conservatory at Alton Towers in
1831 mentions that it was richly ornamented with sculptures, fountains,
piscatories, vases, china jars and cages of singing birds, altogether creating
a most splendid space in which to promenade or idle away the hours. A
watercolour of the circular conservatory at The Deepdene, Surrey, from

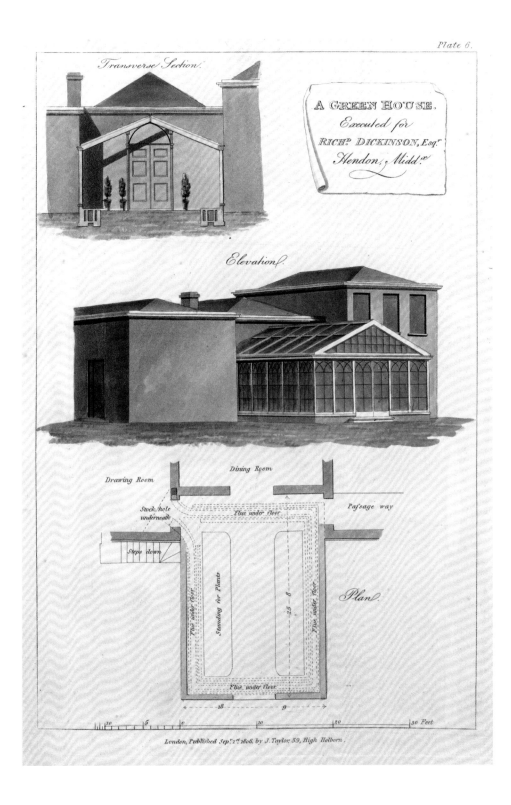

Fig 44 (opposite)
A greenhouse executed for
Richard Dickinson at Hendon,
Middlesex, by George Tod.
[© Royal Botanic Gardens, Kew]

Fig 45
The fishpond in the conservatory
at Belton House. [Melissa
Thompson/National Trust]

1823 shows the profusion of flowers and elegance of furnishings that could render conservatories so delightful (Fig 46). Conservatories were further embellished through the use of coloured or stained glass. Repton's design for a conservatory of 1803 for the Prince Regent at Carlton House (demolished) had a triple-gabled roof creating a space of lofty proportions (Fig 47). A contemporary account of 'a very splendid and imposing conservatory attached to a house on the road to Kensington' describes it as having stained and painted landscapes on the glass which produced 'a most brilliant and imposing effect' when the sun shone through.[89]

Mrs Philip Lybbe Powys' account of her visit in 1796 to Mr Williams' new house, called Temple, near Marlow in Berkshire, shows the degree of opulence and enchantment that conservatories could reach. She describes the house as

> Certainly a very good one, but fitted up and furnish'd in so odd and superb a style, that one cannot help fancying oneself in one of those palaces mention'd in the Arabian Nights' Entertainment ... at the farther end of a most magnificent greenhouse is an aviary full of all kinds of birds, flying loose in a large octagon of gilt wire, in which is a fountain in the centre, and in the evening 'tis illuminated by wax-lights, while the water falls down some rock-work in the form of a cascade. This has a pretty effect, but seems to alarm its beautiful inhabitants, and must be cold for them, I should imagine ... We came away amazingly pleased with having seen so extraordinary a place as Temple must be justly esteem'd.[90]

Plants

As Loudon pointed out, the fashion for conservatories had increased to such a degree that the knowledge and skill needed to stock and manage them did not necessarily keep pace. 'Hence', he wrote, 'it is much more common to see a green-house, than to see one filled with a proper selection of plants in high health and beauty.'[91] He advised that where the conservatory was connected to the drawing room, a 'superior gardener ought to be kept, with abundance of assistance', otherwise the plants would not be in the best condition and this would spoil the effect of the conservatory.[92]

As the employment of a 'superior gardener' was not within the means of all conservatory owners, there was plentiful advice about the most appropriate plants to grow and where to position them. The plants in conservatories were generally grown in beds, as well as in pots, but this practice could be problematic. Plants in beds were able to grow more luxuriously than those restricted by pots, and therefore required pruning. It was also more difficult to remove from a bed an unhealthy plant or one that was out of flower. As a profusion of pots (to the exclusion of beds) could be considered objectionable, an option was to hollow out the floor and cover it in places with ornamental grating instead of paving, to allow larger pots and tubs to be placed under it. If beds were required, it was advised that the conservatory needed to be excavated to about 1m and a drain placed below this depth, covered with broken stones, bricks and so on, and then turf in order to prevent the compost soil from being washed down into the drainage.

Fig 47
The conservatory at Carlton
House, designed in 1803 but
probably not executed. [Royal
Collection Trust/© Her Majesty
Queen Elizabeth II 2019]

Few horticultural catalogues providing lists of available plants survive from this period: out of those printed between 1801 and 1836, there are only 89 extant examples.[93] However, it is still possible to gain a picture of how conservatories were planted from the many other horticultural publications. McIntosh, for example, provides a comprehensive list in *The Greenhouse, Hot House and Stove* (1838), and advises that too many plants of one genus or colour should not be introduced. It was considered especially desirable to choose plants that flower in winter and spring, when there are few opportunities for colour in the garden. If a profusion of blooms all year round was preferred, then free-flowering plants were recommended, and vines and ornamental creepers could be trained up pillars and the underside of rafters. Trees were planted which could provide the illusion of a shrubbery, and fruit trees such as peaches, cherries and figs were also popular. Loudon considered that these imparted an ambrosial appearance, which 'is a great acquisition to a conservatory', and when they grew too large they could be replaced with myrtles, mimosas and other exotics.[94]

Delicate and sun-loving plants were placed at the front of the beds, while those needing less light were placed in the middle or at the back. If the conservatory was heated by fireplaces in the adjoining house then succulents and delicate plants were placed nearby, while the hardiest plants, such as geraniums, roses and hydrangeas, were furthest away. The plants were frequently changed. If it was an option to have a separate hothouse built, then exotics could be brought to perfection before being transferred to the conservatory, and then returned once they were past their bloom. Otherwise, a nurseryman was employed to provide a supply of verdant flowering plants, especially in town gardens, where the fumes from burning coal could prevent plants from thriving. McIntosh gave strict advice that all sickly or deformed plants should be removed from the conservatory, which, 'being the highest in grade of all plant-structures, requires the greatest nicety and care in keeping'.[95]

The benefits of 'indoor gardening'

By the end of the 1830s, conservatories had become well and truly incorporated, structurally and socially, into upper- and middle-class households, providing a highly decorative social space that fused the interior with the garden. It became fashionable for owners to become involved with 'indoor gardening', a pursuit that was invested with notions of gentility as well as with an emerging suburban lifestyle.[96] Loudon wrote that 'a green-house, orangery, or conservatory, ought, if possible, to be attached to every suburban residence'; he saw it as playing a key role in this new domestic ideal, as it allowed women and children to fully participate in the nurture and care of plants.[97]

He anticipated that *The Suburban Gardener* (1838) would afford great enjoyment to ladies and hoped that 'it will tend to the improvement, as far as relates to matters of taste, not only of the gardens under their care, but of the architecture of their house, and of the style and taste of the furniture and finishing of their interiors.' He claimed that

> There is scarcely such a thing to be found as a lady who is not fond of flowers; but it is not saying too much, to affirm that there are very few ladies indeed who are competent to lay out a flower-garden. ... If we can succeed in

rendering every lady her own landscape-gardener, which we are confident we can do, we shall have great hopes of effecting a general reform in the gardening taste, not only of this country, but of every other for which this work is calculated.[98]

As the conservatory was the ladies' domain, its arrangement and care was influential in effecting this reform in gardening taste.

The health resulting from the exercise involved in maintaining a conservatory was seen as a further advantage. Loudon also pointed out the opportunity which a garden or conservatory afforded to its owner of acquiring scientific and practical knowledge.[99] Cushing agreed, observing in *The Exotic Gardener* that 'a conservatory, properly planned, planted, and afterwards well managed, stands forward as a department merely intended for recreation or study, a conspicuous instance of the perfection to which horticulture has arrived in this country.'[100] Great value was placed too on the 'moral effects naturally attending a green-house'. William Cobbett pointed out that there must be amusements in every family, and that as children observe and follow their parents

how much better, during a long and dreary winter, for daughters, and even sons, to assist, or attend, their mother, in a green-house, than to be seated with her at cards, or in the blubberings over a stupid novel, or at any other amusement than can possibly be conceived! How much more innocent, more pleasant, more free from temptation to evil, this amusement, than any other! How much more instructive too![101]

Dr John Lindley, Professor of Botany at the University of London, went even further than this, claiming that 'the love for flowers is a holy feeling, inseparable from our very nature'. He composed a poem on this theme for *Ladies' Botany* (1834) which reads more like a prayer:

O Father, Lord!
The All-Beneficent! I bless thy name,
That thou hast mantled the green earth with flowers,
Linking our hearts to nature! By the love
Of their wild blossoms, our young footsteps first
Into her deep recesses are beguiled,
...
                     By the breath of flowers
Thou callest us, from the city throngs and cares,
Back to the woods, the birds, the mountain streams,
That sing of Thee![102]

The poetry of this period is pervaded with the idea that the study of nature generates moral goodness. Although this notion was not born in the early 19th century, it became more pertinent in an era that saw the beginnings of industrialisation and the growth of cities: nature was increasingly seen as being full of joy and man as being corrupted by civilisation.[103] The suburban garden, in which the conservatory played such a key part, became a refuge from the evils of urbanity in which social and domestic harmony could be achieved.

Afterword

Victorian developments

The construction of Joseph Paxton's Great Stove at Chatsworth in Derbyshire (1836) (Fig 48) began the year before Queen Victoria ascended the throne and neatly marked the transition to a Victorian style of conservatory, heralding the age of the great glasshouses, of which Burton's Palm House at Kew (1848) is another prime example (Fig 49). One of the key differences between Georgian and Victorian conservatories resulted from the increased confidence of architects and manufacturers in working with new materials and their realisation of the potential of iron to span large spaces. The repeal of the glass tax in 1845 and of the window tax in 1851 allowed for more expansive areas of glazing, and in 1847 improvements in glass manufacture by James Hartley created even larger panes unblemished by bubbles or bulges. The invention of a pliable putty using linseed oil meant that these large panes could expand and

contract with much less chance of cracking. Furthermore, the early experiments with hot-water heating were also perfected by the 1840s. The system of using coal-fired boilers to heat hot water which was fed through pipes was both more economical and more efficient than steam heating. Methods of ventilation were also improved, particularly with the invention of the vertical rising ridge system, which allowed for a lantern running along the roof to be opened as a more immediate way of releasing hot air. All these developments and reductions in cost led to the mass production of conservatories (and all types of glasshouses) in the Victorian period.

Alongside the greater scale of conservatories was the ever-increasing desire for growing exotic plants. It is clear from the botanical illustrations of the period how the range of tropical plants available for cultivation in England had expanded, due largely to the travels of those such as Paxton, whose expeditions to India and the Pacific resulted in the availability of 80 new species of orchid. The groundbreaking research of Messrs James Veitch and Sons, the horticultural family whose renowned nurseries were based in Chelsea, and their discovery of rare plants worldwide, fostered the Victorian enthusiasm for horticulture and influenced gardening tastes throughout the 19th century.

Decline

Considering the huge popularity and ubiquity of conservatories in the second half of the 19th century, it is surprising how rarely they were built in the Edwardian period. This was largely due to a change in horticultural fashion and garden design. The highly artificial means of growing exotic plants in conservatories lost favour in the era that idealised the country garden in which perennial plants grew in natural conditions outside. A more open relationship between inside and outside space was desired, and this was more appropriately provided by the loggias and verandas preferred by Arts and Crafts architects.

The First World War also struck a death knell for the conservatory. The loss of so many men from the landowning classes meant there was little chance of new conservatories being commissioned, and the workforce required to maintain existing structures had decreased. Added to this was an increase in the cost of fuel required to heat them. Many conservatories were demolished or became derelict, and by the 1920s the desire for a conservatory had waned considerably.

Guidance for selection for listing

Why list buildings?

The first buildings to be listed were identified soon after the Second World War and there are now just shy of 400,000 entries on the List. The List represents the finest, rarest and historically most innovative buildings in the country as well as those – such as timber-framed cottages, coaching inns and railway stations – that demonstrate how the majority of people have lived and worked over the centuries. Adding a building to the List is a way of celebrating its special interest and protecting what makes it significant by managing any changes to it through the planning system. Listed buildings sometimes need to be sympathetically updated or adapted to keep them viable and in use, and so the vast majority of Listed Building Consent applications are approved.

Fig 48

Paxton's Great Stove at Chatsworth, Derbyshire (1836).

[© Chronicle/Alamy Stock Photo]

What are the criteria for listing Georgian and Regency conservatories?

All buildings are assessed for listing according to the Principles of Selection for Listed Buildings which are set out by the Department for Digital, Culture, Media and Sport. The statutory criteria are the special architectural or historic interest of a building. To be of special architectural interest a building must be of importance in its architectural design, decoration or craftsmanship; to be of special historic interest a building must illustrate important aspects of the nation's social, economic, cultural or military history. There should normally be some quality of interest in the physical fabric of the building itself to justify the statutory protection afforded by listing. Before 1700, all buildings that retain a significant proportion of their original fabric are likely to be regarded of special interest; from 1700 to 1850, most buildings that retain a significant proportion of their original fabric are likely to be regarded of special interest, though some selection is necessary; from 1850 to 1945 progressively greater selection is necessary.

Historic England (which curates the List on behalf of the Secretary of State) publishes a suite of Selection Guides for each building type to indicate the considerations brought to bear when undertaking an assessment. Georgian conservatories are covered in 'Garden and Park Structures', which explains that examples predating 1840, before cheaper glass led to a proliferation of glasshouses, will usually merit listing. The vast majority, if not all, Georgian conservatories on country house estates will already be listed, many at a high grade. In addition to their special interest as architecturally refined and sometimes technologically advanced structures, they make an aesthetic contribution to what is often an ensemble of highly significant buildings. Their presence on such estates, which have had the wherewithal to maintain them, has in many cases ensured their survival.

The Georgian conservatories associated with smaller houses, such as villas or suburban dwellings, have fared less well and are, as a consequence, much rarer. The architectural and historic interest, and potential rarity, of Georgian conservatories renders any example worthy of consideration for listing. The earliest curvilinear structures, or those with surviving evidence of how they were heated, ventilated and even irrigated, may be listable at a high grade. If the main house is already listed, then group value will apply and strengthen the case for listing.

Notes

1   This scene is quoted by Hix 1974, p 90.
2   Loudon 1832, Preface, p v.
3   Loudon 1832.
4   Cushing 1814.
5   Simpson and Weiner 2001, vol III, p 766.
6   Woolsey 1910, vol I, p 217.
7   Tod 1812.
8   Papworth 1818, p 86.
9   Loudon 1835, p 1013.
10   Mrs Loudon 1842.
11   Loudon 1806, p 286.
12   Tod 1812, p 5.
13   Jennings 2005, pp 3 and 59.
14   Repton 1907, p 217.
15   Woods and Warren 1988, pp 89–90.
16   Mackenzie 1818, p 171.
17   Knight 1818.
18   Loudon 1812, p 38.
19   Diestelkamp 1983.
20   Loudon 1835, p 581.
21   Papworth 1818, p 87.
22   Darsie Latimer's description of Joshua Geddes' house in Walter Scott's *Redgauntlet* (1824).
23   Britton and Pugin 1825, pp 84–5.
24   Musson 2005, p 172.
25   Repton 1907, p 217.
26   Ibid.
27   Repton 1907, p 202.
28   Musson 2005, p 172.
29   Papworth 1818, p 85.
30   Loudon 1838, p 414.
31   Loudon 1838, p 111.
32   Loudon 1832, p 6.
33   Britton and Pugin 1825, p 85.
34   McIntosh 1838, p 232.

35   Cushing 1814, p 134.
36   Loudon 1832, p 10.
37   Loudon 1806, p 348.
38   Cobbett 1980, pp 37–8.
39   Loudon 1832, p 7.
40   Papworth 1818, p 86.
41   Loudon 1838, p 110.
42   As Loudon pointed out, though, the atmosphere in London often prevented the healthy growth of plants, so they had to be frequently replaced by jobbing gardeners or nurserymen (Louden 1832, p 216).
43   Brown 1841, p 176.
44   Cushing 1814, pp 134–5.
45   Loudon 1838, p 111.
46   Franklin 1981, p 43.
47   McArthur 1826, p 107.
48   Davidoff and Hall 1991, p 190.
49   Loudon 1832, p 2.
50   *Passages from the Diaries of Mrs Philip Lybbe Powys*, quoted in Girouard 1978, p 234.
51   Lindley 1834, p 2.
52   Mrs Loudon 1840, p 244.
53   Loudon 1818, p 1.
54   Ibid.
55   Loudon 2000, pp 979–80.
56   Loudon 1818, p 1.
57   Papworth 1818, p 85.
58   Ibid.
59   Papworth 1818, p 86.
60   McIntosh 1838, pp 233–4.
61   Loudon 1832, p 12.
62   Kohlmaier 1986, p 27.
63   Loudon 1832, p 13.
64   Pugin 1841, pp 48–9.
65   Loudon 1817, p 48.
66   Loudon 1835, p 581.

67   Loudon 1832, p 21.
68   Loudon 1812, p 45.
69   Cushing 1814, p 134.
70   Loudon 1835, p 1013.
71   Mrs Loudon 1842, p 144.
72   *The Gardener's Magazine* (October 1826).
73   Loudon 1832, p 22.
74   Tod 1812, p 13.
75   Loudon 1832, pp 3–4.
76   Mackenzie 1818, p 176.
77   Loudon 1812, pp 6–7.
78   Loudon 1806, p 348.
79   Loudon 1812, p 39.
80   Tod 1812, pp 6–8.
81   Papworth 1818, p 87.
82   Mickleham 1825, p 325.
83   Abercrombie 1817.
84   Loudon 1806, pp 347–8.
85   Loudon 1838, pp 110–11.
86   Cushing 1814, p 135.
87   Cushing 1814, p 141.
88   Tod 1812, p 11.
89   Brown 1841, p 176.
90   Climenson 1899, pp 2888–9.
91   Loudon 1832, Preface, p v.
92   Loudon 1838, 112.
93   Harvey 1973, p iii.
94   Loudon 1806, p 347.
95   McIntosh 1838, p 241.
96   Longstaffe-Gowan 2001, p 171.
97   Loudon 1838, p 108.
98   Loudon 1838, pp 6–7.
99   Loudon 1838, p 6.
100 Cushing 1814, p 134.
101 Cobbett 1980, pp 39–40.
102 Mrs Lindley 1834, p 3.
103 Day 1996, p 40.

Bibliography

References

Abercrombie, J 1817 'Letter to the Editor' in *Abercrombie's Practical Gardener, or Improved System of Modern Horticulture*. London: T Cadell and W Davies, Strand, p 680

Britton, J and Pugin, A 1825 *Illustrations of the Public Buildings of London*, vol I. London: J Taylor, J Britton and A Pugin

Brown, R 1841 *Domestic Architecture: Containing a History of the Science, and the Principles of Designing Public Buildings, Private Dwelling-Houses, Country Mansions, and Suburban Villas*. London: George Virtue

Climenson, E J (ed) 1899 *Passages from the Diaries of Mrs Philip Lybbe Powys of Hardwick House, Oxon AD 1756 to 1808*. London: Longmans, Green and Co

Cobbett, W 1980 *The English Gardener* (first pub 1829), facsimile of 1833 edn. Oxford: Oxford University Press

Cushing, J 1814 *The Exotic Gardener; in which the Management of the Hot-House, Green-House, and Conservatory is Fully and Clearly Delineated According to Modern Practice*, 3 edn. London: Sherbert, Gilbert and Piper

Davidoff, L and Hall, C 1991 *Family Fortunes: Men and Women of the English Middle Class, 1780–1850*. Chicago, IL: University of Chicago Press

Day, A 1996 *Romanticism*. London: Routledge

Diestelkamp, E J 1983 'Fairyland in London: The Conservatories of Decimus Burton', *Country Life* 19 May 1983, 1342

Franklin, J 1981 *The Gentleman's Country House and its Plan 1835–1914*. London: Routledge and Kegan Paul

Girouard, M 1978 *Life in the English Country House: A Social and Architectural History*. New Haven, CT, and London: Yale

Harvey, J 1973 *Early Horticultural Catalogues: A Checklist of Trade Catalogues Issued by Firms of Nurserymen and Seedsmen in Great Britain and Ireland Down to the Year 1850*. Bath: University of Bath

Hix, J 1974 *The Glass House*. London: Phaidon

Jennings, A 2005 *Georgian Gardens*. London: English Heritage

Kohlmaier, G 1986 *Houses of Glass: A 19th-Century Building Type*. Cambridge, MA: MIT Press

Knight, T A 1818 'Suggestions for the Improvement of Sir George Stuart Mackenzie's Plan for Forcing-houses: Read April 1, 1817'. *Transactions of the Horticultural Society of London* **2**, 350–51

Lindley, J 1834 *Ladies' Botany; or, A Familiar Introduction to the Study of the Natural System of Botany*. London: John Ridway and Sons

Longstaffe-Gowan, T 2001 *The London Town Garden 1740–1840*. New Haven, CT, and London: Yale

Loudon, J C 1806 *A Treatise on Forming, Improving, and Managing Country Residences in two volumes*. London: Longman, Hurst, Rees and Orme

Loudon, J C 1812 *Hints on the Formation of Gardens and Pleasure Grounds with Designs in Various Styles of Rural Embellishment: Comprising Plans for Laying Out Flower, Fruit, and Kitchen Gardens, and the Arrangement of Glass Houses, Hot Walls, and Stoves*. London: John Harding

Loudon, J C 1817 *Remarks on the Construction of Hothouses, pointing out the Most Advantageous Forms, Materials, and Contrivances to be used in their Construction*. London: J Taylor

Loudon, J C 1818 *Sketches of Curvilinear Hothouses; with a Description of the Various Purposes in Horticultural and General Architecture, to which a Solid Iron Sash Bar (Lately Invented) is Applicable*. London

Loudon, J C (ed) 1826–27 *The Gardener's Magazine* (October, April).

Loudon, J C 1832 *The Green-House Companion; Comprising a General Course of Green-House and Conservatory Practice Throughout the Year*, 3 edn. London: Whittaker, Treacher and Co

Loudon, J C 1835 *An Encyclopaedia of Gardening; Comprising the Theory and Practice of Horticulture, Floriculture, Arboriculture, and Landscape-Gardening*, 5 edn. London: Longman, Hurst, Rees, Orme, Brown and Green

Loudon, J C 1838 *The Suburban Gardener and Villa Companion*. London: The author

Loudon, J C 2000 *Encyclopaedia of Cottage, Farm, and Villa Architecture* (first published 1846) reprinted in 2 vols. Shaftesbury: Donhead Publishing Ltd

Loudon, Mrs J 1840 *Instructions in Gardening for Ladies*. London: Murray

Loudon, Mrs J 1842 *The Ladies' Companion to The Flower-Garden*, 2 edn. London: William Smith

Mackenzie, G S 1818 'On the Form which the Glass of a Forcing-house ought to have, in order to receive the greatest possible quantity of Rays from the Sun: By

Sir G S Mackenzie. In a letter to the Right Hon Sir Joseph Banks: Read August 1, 1815'. *Transactions of the Horticultural Society of London* **2**, 176

McArthur P 1826 'Some Account of a Conservatory lately erected at the Grange, the Seat of Alexander Baring, Esq MP Hampshire'. *The Gardener's Magazine*, **1**, 105–115

McIntosh, C 1838 *The Greenhouse, Hot House, and Stove*. London: Wm. S. Orr and Co.

Mickleham, R S 1825 *The Theory and Practice of Warming and Ventilating Public Buildings, Dwelling-Houses and Conservatories*. London: Thomas and George Underwood

Middleton, C 1812 *The Architect and Builder's Miscellany, or Pocket Library; Containing Original Picturesque Designs in Architecture*. London: J Taylor

Musson, J 2005 *How to Read a Country House*. London: Ebury Press

Papworth, J B 1818 *Rural Residences, Consisting of a Series of Designs for Cottages, Decorated Cottages, Small Villas, and other Ornamental Buildings*. London: R Ackermann

Pugin, A W N 1841 *The True Principles of Pointed or Christian Architecture*. London

Repton, H 1840 *The Landscape Gardening and Landscape Architecture of the Late Humphry Repton, Esq Being His Entire Works on These Subjects*, J C Loudon (ed). London: Longman and Co

Repton, H 1907 *The Art of Landscape Gardening, including Sketches and Hints on Landscape Gardening and Observations on the Theory and Practice of Landscape Gardening*, ed J Nolan. London: Archibald Constable and Co

Simpson, J A and Weiner, E S C (eds) 2001 *The Oxford English Dictionary*, 2 edn. Oxford: Oxford University Press

Tod, G 1812 *Plans, Elevations and Sections of Hot-Houses, Green-Houses, An Aquarium, Conservatories etc Recently Built in Different Parts of England, for Various Noblemen and Gentlemen*. London: J Taylor

Woods, M and Warren, A S 1988 *Glass Houses: A History of Greenhouses, Orangeries and Conservatories*. London: Aurum Press

Woolsey, S C (ed) 1910 *The Diary and Letters of Frances Burney, Madame D'Arblay*, 2 vols. London: Little, Brown and Company

Further reading

Batey, M 1995 *Regency Gardens*. Buckinghamshire: Shire

Boniface, P 1982 *The Garden Room*. London: RCHME

Grant, F 2013 *Glasshouses*. Oxford: Shire

Jacques, D 1983 *Georgian Gardens: The Reign of Nature*. London: Batsford

Parissien, S 1995 *The Georgian Group Book of the Georgian House*. London: Aurum Press

2 | Subsequent developments to conservatories and glasshouses and conservation approaches

Fig 50

The Crystal Palace, designed in
1850 by Joseph Paxton (1803–65)
and erected in Hyde Park, London,
seen here in a contemporary
postcard image. The Crystal Palace
was four times the length of St
Paul's Cathedral and Paxton had
just nine days to design in detail a
structure 1,848ft (563m) long and
450ft (137m) wide, with a capacity
of some 33 million cubic feet, using
900,000 square feet of glass, which
was supplied by Chance Brothers of
Birmingham. [© Andrew Fuller]

Introduction

Products and manufacturing techniques for conservatories and glasshouses developed during the 19th century not only generated increasingly sophisticated methods for their construction and operation, but also led to greater understandings of the behaviour of the materials and systems employed, providing valuable data for their subsequent conservation and restoration.

Innovations in the field of industrial chemistry, notably, as Hentie Louw has pointed out,[1] the work of Josiah Wedgwood (1730–1795) and James Keir (1735–1820), led to developments in glass manufacture; advancements in the machine-tool industry, increasing mass production of paints and the mechanisation of brick manufacture led to increasingly sophisticated designs and components for the construction of conservatory and glasshouse structures. The conservatory that Joseph Paxton (1803–65) built at Chatsworth House, Derbyshire, between 1836 and 1841, the Great Stove (*see* Fig 48), covered three-quarters of an acre and was the largest glass structure in the world at the time. It spawned the emergence of an increasing number of conservatory manufacturers, such as Duncan Tucker, Tottenham, London (1830); Richard, Turner, Hammersmith Works, Dublin (1830s); and Foster and Pearson Ltd, Beeston, Nottinghamshire (1841), to service the growing demand.[2]

By 1851, Joseph Paxton had designed the prefabricated glasshouse for the Great Exhibition (Fig 50), a glass and iron leviathan that became a paradigm for wealthy Victorians to replicate, on smaller scales, in urban and country homes across Britain. The demand for conservatories and glasshouses continued to increase throughout the 19th century in response to the fashion for cultivating the exotic and the need to extend the growing season for more ordinary food for home consumption. By 1858, the catalogue (Fig 51) for Messrs Messenger & Co Ltd, Horticultural Builders, Hot Water Engineers and Iron Founders, broadcast that:

Fig 51

Winter garden erected for S B Joel Esq, JP, in Maiden Erlegh, Berkshire, by the architect T H Smith, Esq, from a late 19th-century catalogue by Messenger & Co, Ltd. [Michael Borozdin-Bidnell]

In modern times the cultivation of flowers, exotics etc., has become a distinctive feature of our civilisation and daily life, and there are few who can afford it, who have not their pretty conservatory etc., to brighten and ornament their cottages or mansions. As for the latter it may be said that the conservatory and hothouse forms one of the most attractive and important features of the town or country mansion of the wealthy, and no care or expense is considered too great to make these accessories as perfect and as completely adapted to their surroundings as modern art and science can effect.

The rise of 19th-century manufacturers of mass-produced, standardised conservatories and glasshouses contributed to early- to mid-20th-century restorations of earlier structures. The conservatory at Chiswick House, London, for example, designed by Samuel Ware (1781–1860) had been added by the 6th Duke of Devonshire in 1812–13 and, in 1932–3, after Chiswick House had been sold to Middlesex County Council in 1927, Brentford and Chiswick Urban District Council, to whom the grounds had been leased for use as a public park, undertook major repairs to the conservatory superstructure. The glazed framework, built and modernised by the 6th Duke, was replaced with a patent clear span, post-tensioned steel and timber rafter system by Messenger & Company, with hinged ventilators in place of the previous sliding sashes and cast-iron mullions.

General fundamental guidelines for the conservation of conservatories and glasshouses

Deterioration of ironwork in conservatories and glasshouses can be caused by a number of factors, including overloading, settlement and movement, the impact of mechanical shocks, changes in thermal conditions (such as excessive or rapid heating), corrosion of cast iron, original manufacturing defects, and poorly designed or executed alterations and repairs.

Approaches to the conservation and restoration of conservatories and glasshouses has, as will be seen from the accompanying case studies, varied over the years, but the fundamental aim must be to preserve original fabric wherever possible, and any evidence of traditional design, construction and workmanship should be retained with minimal alteration. Previous repairs should also be retained as found, as long as they prove to be structurally, technically and visually adequate. Consideration should also be given to the replacement of any missing parts and mechanisms which, generally, should not be renewed unless there is sufficiently compelling evidence for their replication, and an appraisal of their implications in terms of future maintenance has been undertaken. It should be noted that varying approaches to the conservation and restoration of conservatories and glasshouses are dependent upon specific and individual site requirements.

It should be remembered that historic structures may not comply with current regulations, standards and codes of practice relating to loadings and structural performance, access, balustrade height and openings, and so on, but, if they are open to the public, health and safety requirements will apply which may conflict with other conservation tenets.[3] The glass in the conservatory at Syon Park, London (Fig 52) – the total frontage of which measures 230ft (70m), the central dome on the tropical house having a diameter of around 40ft (12.2m) – was replaced with toughened safety glass during restoration work carried out between 2014 and 2016, because the building was open to public access.

Fig 52 (opposite)

The conservatory at Syon Park, London. [© Andrew Fuller]

Recording and storage

The first part of the process of any conservation and restoration project must be to record the existing structure. Before commencement of any removal or dismantling, all necessary levels (including levels of primary components and hinges), the locations of fittings such as hinge mountings, and setting-out dimensions must be measured and recorded on drawings to allow the structure to be reinstated or re-erected as found. Surveying levels can reveal settlement and how any movement to the structure may have been accommodated. This recording process should be undertaken at all stages of the work. Once the existing structure has been adequately recorded, the processes of its deterioration should be halted and its condition stabilised. If this is sufficient to ensure the structure's long-term survival, attention should be paid to minimal disturbance of the original materials, employing reversible processes wherever possible.

Strategies that may be employed for this approach include improvement of the immediate environment, which may necessitate appropriate protection from the elements and pollutants, and the use of additional materials or structure, not fixed to the original, to provide further reinforcement, strength or support. In extreme cases this may require relocation to a less destructive environment, if this is the only way in which preservation of the original structure can be ensured.

If repair works are to be undertaken, the structure should only be dismantled as far as is necessary to facilitate repairs or removal and, in general, the sequence of dismantling or removal of components should be the reverse of the order in which they were originally assembled. When dismantling any part of the structure, attention must be paid to the stabilisation of any part-dismantled assemblies in order to prevent any straining of components. Any components that are to be removed from the structure should be tagged with metal tags, wired on and clearly stamped with digits, ideally at least 8mm high, and stored in suitable conditions adjacent to the site; additional tags should be applied as necessary to ensure components are reassembled with their original orientation. Small parts should be bagged together with loose components, tagged, labelled, recorded and secured to the adjacent structure with which they are associated. Original fastenings, such as bolts, nuts and wedges, should be retained for repair and reuse. If any components are rusted or seized together, they should be repeatedly heated and cooled to facilitate their release, taking great care not to overheat thin sections or crack castings. Where possible, fastenings should be returned to their original holes immediately after removal or dismantling.

The first priority should be consolidation and repair of the existing fabric and structure wherever possible, rather than renewal. Traditional materials and techniques should be employed and these should be distinguishable, even on close inspection, from the original fabric. It is important to retain any original parts and materials that are unable to be used in the conservation work, and ideally these should be stored adjacent to or within the structure.[4]

The following sections will discuss the four main conservation areas of conservatories and glasshouses: those of iron and metalwork, glass, woodwork and, perhaps most importantly, surface coatings. The scope of this text does not allow for inclusion of other, equally important aspects of conservatories and glasshouses, such as masonry, heating and ventilating, although these will be addressed where relevant. A final section will look at three new conservatories and some of the issues raised in their planning and construction.

Iron and metalwork

Cast iron

Natural deposits of iron ore, combined with extensive forests from which charcoal could be produced to fuel furnaces, meant that ironwork had become an early component of artefacts for both domestic and commercial use in Britain. From the late 18th century, cast iron had increasingly been commended as a material for the construction of conservatories and glasshouses because of its perceived longevity and ability to provide structural support with far less bulk than equivalent timber-framed structures, thereby allowing more light into the interior of the building. John Henderson, a nurseryman from Brechin, Scotland, wrote, in 1814, that

> Cast-iron is a very advantageous substitute for wood in hot-houses. It is comparably more lasting, its appearance is more light and elegant, and by the proper disposition of columns and screws, rafters are saved, and expense lessened, while all the requisite strength is preserved.[5]

Good-quality cast iron, available from the 1760s onwards, when coke replaced charcoal in the smelting process, produced a more fluid molten metal that could be moulded into increasingly complex patterns (*see* Fig 79).

Humphry Repton (1752–1818) proposed cast iron as the most suitable material for a slender support pillar, in imitation of the 'chapter rooms to some of our cathedrals', to the middle of a planned glasshouse at Plas Newydd, Anglesey, *c* 1800.[6] Repton was clearly a leading advocate for the use of cast iron in building structures, claiming, in a direct reference to the imitation of Gothic elements in buildings, that 'if the architects of former times had known the use we now make of cast iron, we should have seen many beautiful effects of lightness in their works; and surely in ours, we may be allowed to introduce this new material for buildings'.[7]

Cast iron, which could be mass-produced much more economically than wrought iron, contains a relatively high proportion of carbon, distributed throughout the iron in the form of graphite particles. This renders it vulnerable to poor performance under tension, making it a suitable material only for loads carried in compression, such as columns.[8] In the interiors of conservatories and glasshouses it requires relatively little maintenance. But, as old cast iron can be quite brittle, it is more susceptible to physical damage than corrosion. It is also vulnerable to frost damage from trapped water, particularly in rainwater pipes, and rust jacking (where rust expands between components), both of which can cause fractures.

Broken castings can be welded by skilled craftsmen, but, as cast iron can fracture when heated, mechanical repairs such as pinning and stitching (Fig 53) are often preferable. If old iron components are being reused, they should first be warmed to drive out any moisture, and then, as with new components, shot-blasted, using a medium of tiny cast-iron particles, and immediately sprayed with molten zinc, a process known as hot-zinc spraying. Galvanising is not appropriate because cast iron is porous.

New components can be cast using existing elements as patterns. The coefficient of shrinkage in iron is only 1 in 96, so the original

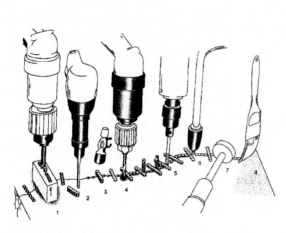

THE PROCESS:

1   A jig is used to drill holes in a line across the crack
2   A pneumatic chisel cuts away part of the webs between holes
3   A steel stitch or lock is hammered in and spreads in the slot
4   Interlocking holes are drilled along the crack
5   Holes are threaded (tapped)
6   Interlocking studs are screwed in
7   Excess metal is dressed off and the surface smoothed
8   Coating is applied

Fig 53

Illustration showing the process

for 'stitching' repairs to cast iron.

[Dorothea Restorations]

pattern must be only fractionally larger than the finished component. Once iron components have been cast, the original methods of machining and preparation are undertaken, the result being that a precise replication is achieved.[9]

The use of cast iron as a suitable material for the construction of conservatories and glasshouses in Britain was eclipsed in the middle of the 19th century, first by wrought iron and, subsequently, steel.[10]

Wrought iron

Unlike cast iron, wrought iron can undergo severe deformation before failure occurs. This is because its carbon content is low (less than 0.08 per cent) which, when fused with approximately 1–2 per cent of fibrous slag, produces a ductile material; an analogy can be made to the way in which the addition of ox hair in decorative plasterwork allows the material to flex without fracturing. Wrought iron performs well in tension, making it particularly suitable for the curved roofs of conservatories and glasshouses.

Metal glazing bars formed from copper alloy had been formed from two or more pieces until 1816, when the Scottish botanist, agriculturalist and architectural writer J C Loudon invented a wrought-iron sash bar, no wider than half an inch, which he presented to the Horticultural Society in May of the same year. Loudon had extolled the virtues of his solid iron sash bar in the *New Monthly Magazine and Universal Register* of 1818, announcing that it had 'great strength and elegance, ... which admits of being bent in every direction without diminishing, but rather increasing its strength'.[11]

When exposed to the elements, wrought iron, like cast iron, corrodes in an electrochemical process, resulting in a layer of hydrated iron oxide (rust), which is porous; this allows the metal to continue to corrode beneath the surface. Although more durable than mild steel, wrought iron is particularly susceptible to corrosion in glazing bars and in those areas that are challenging to paint. The fibrous structure makes it extremely difficult to weld using modern methods (that is, electrically), although the traditional techniques of fire-welding, in which the two components are mechanically fused together while hot, is perfectly satisfactory (Fig 55). Two inherent problems associated with traditional forging techniques are that there are few practitioners with the necessary skills and, unlike mild steel, the building-up of corroded areas is not practical. Mechanical reinforcement may be possible in some instances, but a high degree of replacement is often unavoidable.[12]

Fig 54
Repair to a cast-iron column in the clerestory of the conservatory at Syon Park, by Dorothea Restorations. [Dorothea Restorations]

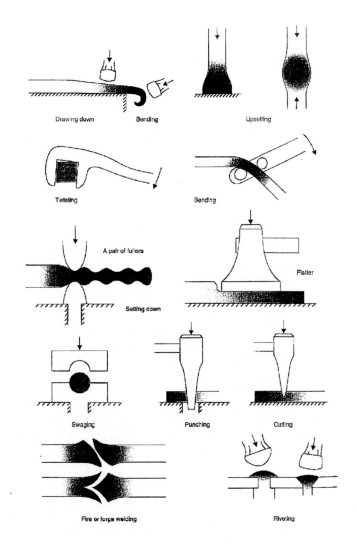

Fig 55
Illustration showing some of the basic blacksmith's forging techniques. [Dorothea Restorations. Geoff Wallis CEng MIMechE]

The glasshouse at Felton Park in Northumberland was restored in 2014–15 by Spence and Dower, Chartered Architects and Historic Building Consultants, Northumberland, with RNJ Partnership Quantity Surveyors, Newcastle upon Tyne (Fig 56).

The lean-to cast- and wrought-iron glasshouse at Felton Park is situated to the east of the house, and includes a potting shed which incorporates an 18th-century garden wall. As Pevsner observed, the glasshouse, believed to have been constructed *c* 1830, displays a 'curved pent roof and fish scale glazing'.[13] Following long neglect, which threatened irreversible decay and destruction, it was included in the English Heritage 2008 North East Region Heritage at Risk Register.

The conservation and restoration of the glasshouse at Felton Park is testament to concerted effort by an enthusiastic owner, with support from Historic England, the Heritage Lottery Fund (HLF), the Country Houses Foundation and Northumberland County Council. A trial project was established in 2014 to examine the possible scope of the work, inform the technical requirements of the project, and establish an affordable conservation strategy that would respect the integrity of both the iron frame and the historic glass. This investigative trial, which focused upon a single section of the vertical cast-iron frame and a corresponding area of the lower part of the curved roof (Fig 57), determined that the quality of this glasshouse suggested that it was the product of an established manufacturer who was capable of the design, fabrication and assembly of the iron components to a high standard.

Fig 56

The greenhouse at Felton Park, Northumberland. [Spence and Dower Architects]

Fig 57

An investigative trial to a single section of the vertical cast-iron frame and a corresponding area of the lower part of the curved roof at Felton Park. [Spence and Dower Architects]

The plan of the glasshouse measures approximately 30m × 5.25m, abutting the 18th-century garden wall, which rises to a height of 5m at this point. The glazing bars of the pent roof are of wrought iron, leaded into sockets formed in the back wall of a gutter above a cast-iron frame, which, on the south front, is seated on a low stone plinth wall, and contains top-hung casement ventilators. The glasshouse is ventilated at the top of the pent roof by a raised parapet of the brick wall through which shafts rise to dispersal grilles fixed within each face of the wall just below the coping, ventilation being controlled by hinged panels to the shafts, each operated by a pulley with a finely balanced counterweight (Fig 58).

Fig 58

An illustration showing ventilation grilles at the top of the pent roof at Felton Park. [Spence and Dower Architects]

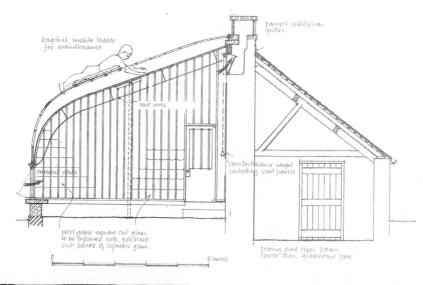

Fig 59

Wrought-iron glazing bars of the curvilinear roof, which are grouted in with lead to the cast-iron vertical frame. [Spence and Dower Architects]

The design of the glasshouse at Felton Park is an example of how both cast and wrought iron have been adapted to take advantage of their specific properties and performance under stress. Cast iron was used for the frame of the vertical south wall, components having been assembled and bolted together as a series of identical panels, combining compressive strength with rigidity. The cast-iron cill is bedded on to the stone plinth and the head of the frame includes a substantial gutter, cast with sockets in the top of the back edge of the section housing the ends of the fine-rolled, wrought-iron glazing bars of the curvilinear roof, which are grouted in with lead (Fig 59). The slender wrought-iron glazing bars, with very narrow rebates for the roof of the glasshouse, facilitate the steep curvilinear slope at Felton Park. This design provides the structure with strength at right angles to the glass panes but does not offer any resistance against horizontal distortion, a function performed by the glass panes themselves, which, once inserted, form a rigid diaphragm between the bars.

Loudon, in his *Encyclopaedia of Cottage, Farm and Villa Architecture and Furniture* (1833), cites this particular function of the glass panes in conservatories and glasshouses in reference to the great conservatory at Bretton Hall, West Yorkshire (Fig 60), built in 1827 but dismantled and sold by 1832. The reliance solely on the wrought-iron sash bars, without either rafters or principal ribs for additional support of the structure, was a cause for some anxiety

for when the ironwork was put up, before it was glazed, the slightest wind put the whole of it in motion from the base to the summit. As soon as the glass was put in however it was found to become perfectly firm and strong, nor did the slightest accident from any cause happen to it from the time it was completed till it was sold and taken down.[14]

The curvilinear span of the roof at Felton Park, 6m long, has an additional central purlin, now a mild steel angle, but formerly believed to have been made from cast iron, with spandrels supported on slender columns. Four drawn wrought-iron wires, equally spaced in the slope of the roof, and running the whole length of the glasshouse, are threaded through holes in the webs of the wrought-iron glazing bars. They are lightly tensioned with turnbuckle joints, and, even though they are not welded in place, serve to prevent any glazing bar from springing out of line.

Repeated wetting and freezing had lifted much of the fillet putty and paint, allowing water to penetrate the wrought-iron glazing bars and causing rusting of the ironwork (Fig 61). This had led to severe corrosion of the section of the bars

Fig 60
An illustration showing the Great Conservatory at Bretton Hall, West Yorkshire, built by W & D Bailey of London.

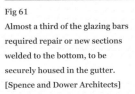

Fig 61
Almost a third of the glazing bars required repair or new sections welded to the bottom, to be securely housed in the gutter.
[Spence and Dower Architects]

74

immediately above the cast-iron frame, in many places leading to a loss of their cross-sectional strength. New wrought-iron sections were rolled and welded *in situ* on to the cut bars, then grouted into their original sockets with molten lead (Figs 62 and 63).

The vertical cast-iron casement frames in the south wall, consisting of flat sections of cill, with a flange along the underside set into a continuous chase cut into the top of the projecting stone cill along the dwarf wall (*see* Fig 63), had originally been plugged and screwed into the stone, but this fixing had rusted away. This problem was augmented because the seating of the cast-iron cill had become completely open and the nosing of every piece of stone cill had been forced out of place, split off by the freezing of water trapped in the chase. The glazed casements were removed to the contractor's workshop at the beginning of the project and were only refitted following completion of the repairs to the

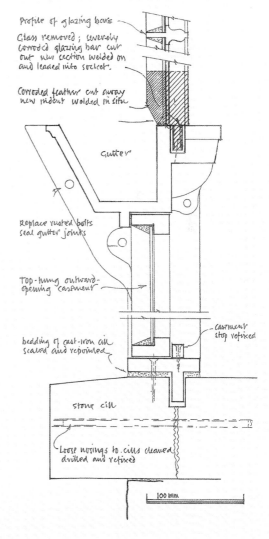

Fig 62 (above)

New wrought-iron sections were rolled and welded *in situ* onto the cut bars, then grouted into their original sockets with molten lead. [Spence and Dower Architects]

Fig 63 (right)

A section detail through the front cast-iron frame showing repairs. [Spence and Dower Architects]

Fig 64
Most of the nosings of the stone cill to the plinth, split off through the action of ice, were clamped, drilled and refixed with 8mm stainless steel threaded bars which were drilled deep into each face and filled with epoxy resin adhesive. [Spence and Dower Architects]

Fig 65 (below left)
Cast-iron corner posts which served as rainwater downpipes from the front gutter had become blocked and split. [Spence and Dower Architects]

Fig 66 (below)
The recast corner post with downpipe terminates in an open lead shoe above a gulley draining to a soakaway at each corner. [Spence and Dower Architects]

masonry. This consisted of reinforcing the loose nosings to the cill by cleaning off the faces of the longitudinal split beneath the cast-iron cill and bonding the nosing back to the undisturbed stone behind using 8mm stainless steel threaded bars drilled deep into each face and filled with epoxy resin adhesive (Fig 64).

The posts supporting the casement frames were housed in prepared slots at the joints of the cast-iron cill sections, and the gutters, each spanning two bays of the frame, were bolted together across the posts with lead gaskets and putty jointing, the only running outlets being the two hollow cast-iron end posts. Although the level gutter had capacity enough for most rainfall, the corner posts, being constricted in cross-section and connected to below-ground drainage with no access for clearance, had backed up with water which had frozen, causing both posts to split and leak (Fig 65). The posts proved to be beyond repair and so were removed, new patterns being made from which castings were prepared for reinstatement. To facilitate easy cleaning and avoid blockage, a change in the detail of the posts was implemented so that the downpipe terminated in an open lead shoe above a gulley, draining to a soakaway at each corner (Fig 66).

Hollow cast-iron structural supports in conservatories and glasshouses were often used as downpipes for rainwater. Charles McIntosh describes the practical advantages of the use of this system in the conservatory at The Grange in Hampshire (Fig 67)

> The roof ... is supported by cast-iron hollow columns, which also carry off the water which falls on the roof, into drains properly placed for its reception ... and in which, after supplying an immense reservoir under the ground for the supply of the house, as well as for use in the event of fire, or any other scarcity of water, empties the remainder beyond the limits of the buildings.[15]

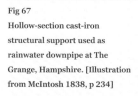

Fig 67

Hollow-section cast-iron structural support used as rainwater downpipe at The Grange, Hampshire. [Illustration from McIntosh 1838, p 234]

In assessing repairs to cast and wrought iron, consideration should be given to how the building was assembled, and how it was intended to work structurally: which members, for instance, are primary, and therefore critical in load-bearing, and which are secondary and decorative. An analysis should be carried out to assess which members are subject to tensile, compressive and compound stresses, and an assessment of how the structure is currently working should also be undertaken. Attention should also be addressed to the condition of each element, particularly vulnerable components, such as footings, fastenings, water traps, water pipes and columns, thin castings, crevices and joints, splash zones, interlocking parts and associated materials.[16]

Reassembly or reinstatement

Ironwork should be reassembled or reinstated precisely in its original location, reusing original fastenings, providing they are in good condition and sufficiently strong. New fastenings should be galvanised to match the originals, with their imperial threads. Care must be taken to avoid straining the ironwork as the joints are pulled together.

The Fernery glasshouse in the Swiss Garden (Fig 68) was restored in 2013–14 by Eura Conservation Ltd, with associated building work by Fairhurst Ward Abbotts Ltd and conservation of Pulhamite artificial rockwork by Simon Swan Associates. The £330,000 HLF-funded project was carried out under the supervision of conservation architect Chris Garrand, working with historic metalwork consultant Geoff Wallis and structural engineer Ed Morton.

The Swiss Garden is a rare survival of Regency landscape design, originally planned by Lord Robert Ongley (1803–77) *c* 1830. Ongley, who had inherited Old Warden Park in 1814, transformed a 9-acre (3.6ha) section of boggy brickfield in north-east Bedfordshire into an alpine scene, a great earth-moving feat, moulding a level patch of land into an undulating landscape complete with mounds, ponds, serpentine paths and shrubberies, including a Swiss Cottage, an aviary (lost) and a grotto-cum-fernery. A complex building, the basic plan and form of the Grotto and Fernery can, due to the fabrication of the ironwork by the short-lived Northampton firm of Barwell & Hagger, be accurately dated to 1830–33, albeit documentary evidence reveals the current dome to have been provided in 1877 by the Norwich firm of Barnard & Bishop.

Ongley left Old Warden in the early 1850s, after which the Swiss Garden fell into decline, but it was restored between 1876 and 1880 by the industrialist Joseph Shuttleworth (1819–83). Sale particulars of 1872 describe the building at that time as a 'domed and arched conservatory approached through a grotto, the Roof constructed of iron and being heated with hot water'. Following acquisition by Shuttleworth, substantial work was undertaken, between 1876 and 1878, to the structure of the Fernery, when it was extensively restored and reglazed. After the Second World War, the Swiss Garden once again fell into decline but, during the 1970s, derelict and vandalised, an extensive programme of repair and renewal was begun, leading, in the early 21st century, to an almost complete reglazing of the Fernery in float glass. However, due to lack of investment and an uncertain future, the Swiss Garden, a major element of the, by now, Grade II* registered Old Warden Park, was, in 2009, placed on the English Heritage at Risk Register, leading to a £3.6 million restoration funded by HLF, the Country Houses Foundation, the Shuttleworth Trust, Central Bedfordshire Council and others.

The glasshouse Fernery in the Swiss Garden is set on an east–west axis, with wrought-iron vaults rising from cast-iron clerestories on low brick walls; cast-iron spandrels and columns add support. At the crossing is a brick drum supporting the dome, with a timber cupola rising to a gilded finial. The metalwork of the glasshouse at the Swiss Garden is a precision mix of wrought and cast iron, with much of the original 1830s and 1870s fabric surviving. One particularly important survival is a number of hooks and other details believed to be historically associated with early shading methods in the form of external blinds that could be pulled down to gutter level, probably by way of chain-operated drive shafts at the ends nearest the dome. Decorative central, ridge-level castings at each end of the wings are believed to be the end plates of the roller mechanism, with the attached curved wrought-iron rails running down to the gutters being guides. Remnants of small fastenings on the lips of the gutters below may be the lower fixings of missing guide rails, and hooks just below the gutters and along the leading edges of the gables may have been for hanging curtains over the vertical surfaces.

Fig 68

The Grotto and Fernery at the Swiss Garden, Bedfordshire. [CT AABC, © Stephanie Foote 2014]

Built for the nurturing of ferns and alpine plants, the interior of the glass Fernery is inherently damp: an aggressive environment in which to conserve historic ironwork, especially the very slender sections of the glazing bars (ribs) which make up the vaulted roofs (Fig 69). Relative humidity was data-logged, recording, in general, an excess of 90 per cent, and detailed inspection revealed corrosion to over forty of the glazing bars, most seriously where the ends sat in lead-caulked sockets integral to the cast-iron gutters, and, to a lesser extent, at the ridge purlins (Fig 70). Corrosion had also weakened the base of the dome, the original wrought-iron ribs (a different section to the vaults and pitted with holes) having, in the 1970s, been welded to a mild steel ring that was heavily rusted, a situation not helped by the whole dome resting only on plastic packers sitting in puddles of water. Cast-iron elements of the Fernery wings were in good

Fig 69

Glazing bars to the vaulted rooves.

[© Stephanie Foote 2014]

Fig 70

Corroded ridge purlins.

[© Stephanie Foote 2014]

condition, except for cracks in two places, and some fractures at the hinge points of the casements, many of the hinges being corroded.

Early in the project it was decided that conservation of the glass Fernery should be driven by a desire that its historic usage should continue, even though this would mean promoting a damp, corrosive internal environment. Decisions on repair, conservation and restoration therefore had to be made on the basis of a thorough understanding of the interaction between temperature, humidity and air movement, in order to avoid premature failure of potentially vulnerable ironwork.

Float glass of the 1970s was removed and it became clear that the state of the slender and precise wrought-iron glazing bars, which had largely survived intact since their fabrication in the early 1830s, necessitated extensive conservation work. Cleaning the ironworks revealed their true state and the need for repairs; while little repair was needed to cast elements (cracks were plated *in situ*), in order to ensure that the rebates on the wrought-iron ribs would provide a suitable platform for the glazing, extensive filling, fettling (trimming and cleaning of the rough edges) and linishing (grinding to improve flatness) was required to both original and poorly executed modern welds. A number of ribs were removed, repaired and re-rolled, with two renewed entirely in wrought iron. Non-structural holes were made good by brazing, the relatively low temperatures involved allowing filler to flood the voids without overheating the iron, and the badly corroded or distorted ends of wrought-iron glazing bars were renewed, making use, where possible, of sections salvaged from two that had been discarded because of their extreme deterioration. An epoxy putty filler was used to fill porosity in castings, gaps in joints, cracks and water traps.[17] The dome was dismantled and taken to the workshop for repair, along with all the cast-iron casements. Cracks in the latter were welded and new bespoke brass hinges made to fit the historic mortices, imperial fixings being used throughout. New details (Fig 71) were developed to ensure a positive, durable fixing for the base of the dome and to weather the almost flat crowns of the Fernery vaults.

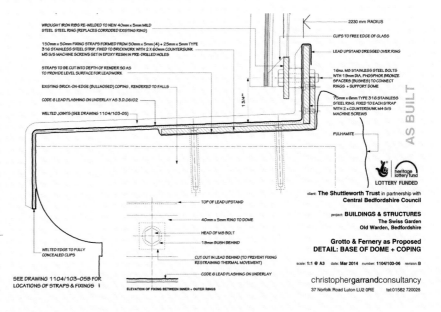

Fig 71
New details at the base of the dome. [Christopher Garrard Consultancy]

The conservatory at Hilton Park (Fig 72) was restored by Hilton Hall Limited under the direction of the architect Tim Ratcliffe of Oswestry. Geoff Wallis was metalwork consultant. The repairs were carried out under the JCT Intermediate Building Contract (IC 11) and took 21 months to complete at a cost of £292,000. The project was completed in March 2015.

The conservatory at Hilton Park is situated approximately 90m to the north-west of Hilton Hall, which was converted for office use in the latter part of the 20th century. The nucleus of the Hilton Park Estate – contracted in size over many years, with land sold off incrementally or purchased for the construction of the M6 and M54 motorways, and the Hilton Park service station – survives in the form of the partly moated 18th-century house, a stable block and a walled garden. The location of the conservatory is identified on the 1888 edition of the Ordnance Survey map, and the structure must have been clearly visible to the hall across the moat: it was evidently a feature in the designed landscape surrounding the hall and, given its relatively distant location from the walled garden, designed for ornament rather than mere utility.

While subsequent research revealed a great deal about the development of the Hilton Park Estate and the fortunes of the families that created it, there was surprisingly little found about the conservatory itself. One illustration discovered, thought to date from *c* 1795 (Fig 73) shows a pedimented building in the same location relative to the hall itself. Correspondence with illustrations from 1818 refers to a half-round glasshouse (Fig 74) with the same roof profile, comparable to the earlier building.

Fig 72

The conservatory at Hilton Park, Staffordshire. [© Historic England/ John Tiernan]

Fig 73
Illustration *c* 1795 showing a pedimented garden building relative to Hilton Hall. [By kind permission of B F R Vernon; photo Cherry Ann Knott]

Fig 74
An 1818 illustration of a half-round glasshouse at Hilton Hall. [By kind permission of B F R Vernon; photo Cherry Ann Knott]

This fascinating garden building had been on the Historic England Heritage at Risk Register since it was launched in 2008 and, by December 2011, was in a dire state of repair (Fig 75). It appeared not to have been used or maintained in any meaningful way for several decades and was practically at the point of collapse. The cast-iron structure generally was compromised by extensive corrosion and rust jacking[18] (Fig 76), with numerous fissured or

Fig 75

The conservatory in 2001.

[© Historic England/John Tiernan]

Fig 76

Extensive corrosion and rust jacking. [© Historic England/ John Tiernan]

broken components. Most of the glass panes were missing, the glazed timber roof had collapsed and the brickwork arches to the central flue were supported by temporary timber centring on scaffolding (Fig 77).[19] Most of the building was heavily colonised by ivy and other vegetation (Fig 78). Nevertheless, the conservatory appears to be unique by virtue of its shape and the combination of traditional and new building materials employed. While the method of space-heating used predates developments in low-pressure hot-water heating systems, the building was clearly at the forefront of technological development; those involved with its subsequent repair had not encountered a similar freestanding structure elsewhere.

The proposal to comprehensively repair the conservatory was facilitated by a substantial Historic England repair grant in 2012, following a grant application made on behalf of the owners. This had been supported by a detailed condition survey of the cast-iron structure prepared by Geoff Wallis of GW Conservation, but nothing was discovered about the building's history. The prescribed investigation works set out in the grant offer were therefore included to facilitate an understanding of the building within the context of the landscape, to secure detached or loose parts of the building fabric, and to try to find out as much as possible about the masonry and subterranean construction in order to inform the repairs specification.

Fig 77

Timber centring supporting brickwork arches and the central flue. [© Historic England/ John Tiernan]

Investigation works to inform the repairs specification were deemed invaluable at Hilton Park, and the grant from Historic England allowed for a measured survey to be made of the structure, a detailed photographic survey, site clearance to facilitate repair operations, and the collection of all detached or loose components and storage until required.[20] The project team was very clear from the start that it was key to understand how the conservatory had been assembled originally in order to dismantle it and undertake the necessary repairs. The first site meeting was attended by all the professionals involved, the main contractor and subcontractors, and the exact sequence of dismantling agreed in principle and confirmed by method statements. The building was recorded digitally in order to provide basic as-existing drawings.

Although the conservatory at Hilton Park is a relatively simple building in concept, it is remarkably sophisticated in its construction. Built on a raised stone plinth that projects beyond the line of its external wall, it is circular on plan, approximately eight metres in diameter. The roof, constructed in two halves, and separated by a brick dividing wall above eaves level, is carried by two arches and supported by a central brick column. The conservatory is open on plan and configured on a north-east–south-west axis in which the south-west side is constructed almost entirely of cast iron and glass, and the north-east side render-covered brick walls and a timber glazed roof.

Excavations around the perimeter of the building revealed the remains of a straight brick wall which had nothing to do with the existing building but may have been related to the earlier pedimented building. While the geometrical form of the conservatory is convincing enough, the physical division between traditional timber and masonry construction for one half of the structure, and cast/wrought iron for the other, suggests either lack of vision or a loss of nerve. On the other hand, its general symmetry, and the configuration of heating ducts beneath the floor and its central flue, suggest that it is a considered design and not something that has been changed mid-way through building. A plausible explanation could be that the conservatory followed existing precedents, in which a glasshouse was invariably a lean-to structure adjacent to a traditional masonry building, and that the building represents a transitional development in glasshouse technology.

The metalwork is almost all prefabricated cast iron of high quality, using the smallest of sections to achieve the largest spans. Applied classical detail, in the form of antefixa, with a frieze of honeysuckle fixed to the top of the gutter and a Greek key on the inside face of the wall plate (Fig 79), suggests a construction date of the early 19th century, probably between 1800 and 1830. There are no visible signs of the manufacturer's name or a casting date.

The south-west side contains the principal entrance, which projects forward from the perimeter wall and has a triangular pediment supported by slender, hollow rectangular section cast-iron pilasters with applied composite capitals (*see* Fig 72). The flanking curved walls are divided into four bays by the same type of pilasters, which rise from a hollow section, cast-iron sill plate to support a cast-iron wall plate with an integral combined external gutter and internal condensation channel. Each of the bays has a casement of 20 glazed panels, only the end two panels having a single copper-framed opening light in the top row of four panes, indicating that ventilation, at this level at least, does not appear to have been a significant consideration.

Fig 79
The Greek key detail to the inside
face of the wall-plate. [© Historic
England/John Tiernan]

The roof over the south-west side consists of 11 curved ribs of very slender proportions (110 × 50mm) that divide the roof into 10 equal segments, each of which is aligned with the pilasters below. These converge on the crown, where a cornucopia-like pendant once filled the space below the connecting ring beam. Each segment is subdivided vertically into seven sections by moulded glazing bars, formed from folded and profiled sheets of copper alloy and secured with two equally spaced transverse iron bars to provide lateral stability, at least two of which span the same distance as the main ribs, but are barely 13mm wide and 25mm deep. Glazing to the longest of these sub-segments consists of approximately 23 rectangular quarries of clear glass, which were overlapped to provide a weatherproof covering. The existing glass is believed to have been clear cylinder glass, 1–2mm thick, but it had become discoloured and soiled over time.

The roof structure to the north-east side is similar in concept to that on the south-west but is largely executed in timber. The perimeter walls are constructed in brickwork, plastered internally, and rendered externally to form a façade of four blind panels to either side of a pair of north-east-facing doors diametrically opposed to the south-west entrance. Prior to repair, the whole of this roof structure had become detached, had slid off the wall en masse, and was propped precariously against it (Fig 80). It was still more or less intact as a complete structure and consisted of eight primary ribs (125 × 75mm) dividing the roof into ten equal segments; these were subdivided into four by three secondary ribs of lesser section (50 × 50mm) secured by equally spaced transverse iron bars in the same manner as the south-west roof. The second, fourth, seventh and ninth segments had top-hung opening lights at wall plate level, which were rectangular in shape and divided by three vertical glazing bars (Fig 81). The glass quarries used here were almost twice as wide as those used on the south-west side but none appeared to have survived the partial collapse. Nothing remained of the curved wall plate but it was evident that it had originally been

Fig 80
The north-east roof structure
propped precariously against the
central brick structure. [© Historic
England/John Tiernan]

Fig 81
Top-hung opening lights to the
north-east roof. [© Historic
England/John Tiernan]

located on the outer face of the wall, where several of the holding-down bolts were still in place. Displaced cast-iron gutters fixed to the outer face of the wall plate had similar profiles to those integral with the wall plate on the south-west side. Only a single leaf of two flush panels remained of the north door together with parts of the frame; the door was framed by timber pilasters and flush with the outer face of the wall.

The central column within the conservatory was surrounded by tiered brick staging, presumably for displaying potted plants and other flora. As this occupied a considerable part of the floor area, was a much later insertion, and its weight was causing the floor to settle, it was agreed that it should be removed. The stone floor beneath was found to be largely intact and repairable. The brick staging had been built around the fluted column and profiled base; this had protected the gypsum and lime plaster profiles, therefore enabling recreation of what had been lost above (Figs 82–84).

Fig 82

The stone floor. [© Historic England/John Tiernan]

Fig 83

The base of the central column. [© Historic England/John Tiernan]

Fig 84
The completed interior.
[© Historic England/John Tiernan]

While acknowledging the sheer elegance of the cast-iron structure, derived from the slender proportions of its component parts and the large spans accommodated, the manner of its construction appeared to ignore the basic tenets of good building practice. Because of the accumulated detritus within the gutter, corrosion and the general state of disrepair, it was initially difficult to ascertain how the metal components were assembled. Once access to start dismantling was provided, it soon became evident that the end of each principal rib sat in the perimeter gutter (Figs 85 and 86) above each of the wall frame posts, with the whole assembly connected by a wrought-iron rod with threaded ends; this extended from the rib foot to the sill plate of the wall frame, the

Fig 85
The principal ribs seated in the perimeter gutter pr ior to restoration. [© Historic England/ John Tiernan]

Fig 86
Principal ribs seated in the perimeter gutter following restoration. [© Historic England/ John Tiernan]

whole held in compression by a square nut at each end (Fig 87). To allow one
of the main structural elements of the building to be covered by water seems
incredulous enough – water would only drain when the level exceeded the obstacle
created by the rib foot – but the gutter had only one 50mm-diameter opening
at one end of the gutter, which connected into a lead pipe of the same diameter
concealed behind the rendered surface of the adjoining brick wall. Both gutter
opening and pipe were completely filled by ivy roots and vegetation and had
clearly contributed to the failure of the building once regular maintenance ceased.

Surprisingly, most of the cast-iron components had survived in place, albeit
with stress fractures and distortion through rust jacking, but nothing that could
not be addressed by welding and/or augmentation with new castings. The
overall form had inevitably become distorted and putting it back to how it was
originally would have been almost impossible. Some adjustment might have
been possible, but it would have to be within the limits of those reference points
established by the floor plan and the adjoining brick walls.

The process of dismantling, inspection, cleaning, repair and redecoration
prior to reassembly was relatively straightforward (Fig 88). It was always
taken for granted that repairs to the cast-iron components would be carried
out off-site and that the standing masonry and floor would be protected by a
scaffolded enclosure for the duration of the contract. This did not happen, but
the main contractor provided an assortment of protective measures (Fig 89) to
keep all the other works dry and under cover while progressing on other areas of
construction, and kept the costs within budget.

The previous method of discharging collected rainwater was clearly
totally inadequate and so the guttering to both roofs was extended into two
diametrically opposed hoppers, each with a cast-iron downpipe and a shoe
discharging over a gully set below the stone plinth (Figs 90 and 91). As thieves
had stolen several of the copper glazing bars during the dismantling process,
metal theft was a major consideration and it was decided, after much debate,
not to reinstate lead. For this reason, terne-coated stainless steel sheet was used
to cover the margin between the cast-iron and timber roofs; even the rainwater
hoppers were formed in timber and lined with fibreglass.

Fig 88
Dismantling the structure.
[© Historic England/John
Tiernan]

Fig 89
Protective measures. [© Historic
England/John Tiernan]

Conservation of the conservatory at Syon Park (Fig 92) was undertaken by Dorothea Restorations, under the supervision of the estates personnel, head gardener Topher Martyn, consultant architect Dannatt Johnson Architects, and structural engineers Cooper and Withycombe from 2015 to 2017.

Henry Percy, the 9th Earl of Northumberland, acquired the former monastic house of Syon in 1597, since when it has remained in the same family. In 1827, the 3rd Duke of Northumberland commissioned the architect Charles Fowler (1791–1867) to design the Great Conservatory in grounds that had been laid out by Capability Brown. The total frontage measures 230ft (70.1m) and the central dome on the tropical house has a diameter of around 40ft (12.2m).

In April 2012, a survey of the structure of the conservatory at Syon Park was commissioned, following observation by the estates staff of rusting and loss and failure of mastic and silicone pointing which had been applied during previous decorative works to the building. A previous survey had been undertaken in July 1984 and the 2012 survey revealed that, due to failure of the decorative systems to the cast-iron arches and girders to the base of the dome, the joints between the components had begun to open up, allowing water to enter the voids and accumulate on the inverted channel sections and within hollow sections (Fig 93). The construction detail of a high-level access gantry at the base of the

Fig 92

The conservatory at Syon Park, London. [Andrew Fuller]

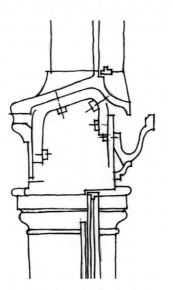

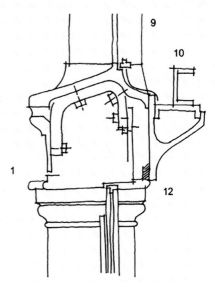

Fig 93
Sections showing the 'original'
gutter detail at the base of the
dome, indicated by the 1984 survey
of the Great Conservatory at Syon
Park, which was replaced during
the 1980s repair programme
with one of a larger section which
carries the high-level access
gantry installed at this time.
[Dannatt Johnson Architects]

Secion 1-1

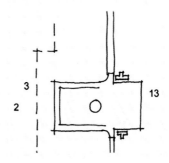

dome effectively prevented access to properly maintain the decorative finishes to the gutter as well as the joints between the components of the construction, and this had to be temporarily removed to allow full repairs to be carried out.

The vertical glazing comprises fairly conventional timber sash windows, albeit with brass glazing bars. The main problems were excessive rusting to glazing frame support pins. These were removed and new ones forged then drilled and tapped into the existing location. Historic repairs that had been poorly carried out, that is, plates that had not been coated properly and were now jack rusting, were removed and redone. In two locations there were cracks to structural columns due to movement; these were metal stitched and plated (see Fig 53). The plates were fully painted and bedded on a suitable sealant.

During the first phase of the recent repair work, advantage was taken of the opportunity to carry out some investigative work, including the disassembly of part of the iron ring beam. Although there was some rusting and deterioration of the metalwork, there was little loss of material and the underlying structure was not badly affected. Connecting bolts showed more sign of decay, and these were generally replaced where access was possible. There was also some localised splitting of the ironwork, probably caused by the members being too slender to resist buckling caused by wind load. These were repaired by metal stitching. Some strengthening of the original construction, through the installation of additional cleats and straps, had been undertaken during the 1980s following the 1984 survey, and this had proved effective.

The conservatory at Alton Towers (Fig 94) was restored *c* 1980, as part of the then owners' programme of restoration of historic features and garden buildings on this great estate. The architects were Donald Insall Associates.

This remarkable and handsome conservatory, some 230ft (70.1m) in length, and one of the buildings erected by the 15th and 16th Earls of Shrewsbury, had been designed by Robert Abraham (1774–1850) in 1818. A private company had purchased the estate from the Shrewsbury family in 1924, being re-formed as Alton Towers Limited after the Second World War, during which time the estate had been occupied by the army.

The building, constructed from Hollington stone, a red Triassic sandstone from Staffordshire, carries seven glazed cast-iron domes, all of which had suffered extensive deterioration, all being severely rusted, with many of their ornamental crestings and decorative ironwork features missing or removed for munitions during the Second World War. The roof leadwork also demanded extensive repair, and the stonework, particularly the console brackets, had been split by rusting iron cramps.

The work (Fig 95) to the conservatory at Alton Towers demonstrates how approaches to conservation and restoration have changed during the last 50 years. By 1975, the glass domes (Figs 96 and 97) to the monumental conservatory were in a dilapidated condition. All of the original timber roof lights had suffered extensively from wood rot by the time of its restoration between 1975 and 1980, and, in the central pavilion, the external curved stone cornice had cracked and dropped, due to the failure of the cast-iron

Fig 94

The conservatory at Alton Towers, Staffordshire. [Donald Insall & Associates Architects]

Fig 95 (opposite)

Axonometric showing repairs. [Donald Insall & Associates Architects]

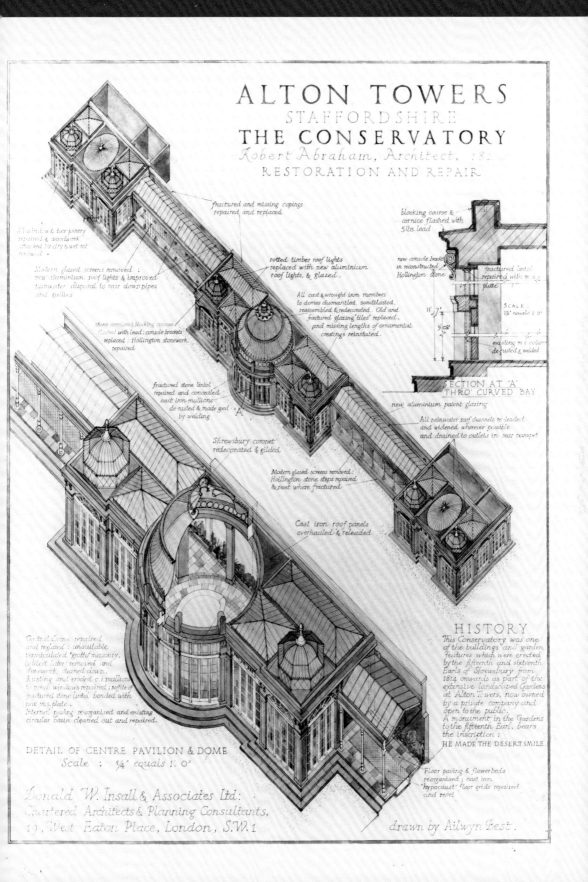

intermediate supports between the piers, which had rusted, forcing the surrounding joinery apart. The decision was taken at the time to replace them with aluminium sections, to a profile and module harmonising with the original work.

Repair work began in September 1975, when the glazing was removed, and all of the cast-iron frames were dismantled in sections, thoroughly descaled and de-rusted by shot-blasting. The cast-iron sections were then reassembled using non-ferrous bolts, treated with a rust-inhibiting primer and reglazed with small squares of Pilkington's float glass in a special mastic. In the central pavilion, with its large dome, most of the eight cast-iron stays, which supported the main ribs, had rusted so badly that they had to be replaced, the work being undertaken by a local blacksmith. The lantern, with its concave pivoted lunettes and the distinguishing Shrewsbury coronet, was coloured and gilded, its lunettes being filled with copper gauze to provide permanent ventilation. Missing lengths of cresting were replaced in aluminium around the dome and new drainage weep holes were provided.

The conservation programme at Alton Towers earned a Civic Trust Commendation in 1982.

Fig 96
Dilapidation of the domes.
[Donald Insall & Associates
Architects]

Fig 97

Dilapidation of the domes.

[Donald Insall & Associates

Architects]

Glass

Cylinder, or broad, and crown glass methods of handmade flat glass manufacture survived in Britain until the 20th century. Broad sheet glass, made by blowing molten glass into an elongated balloon shape, was first produced in Britain early in the 12th century. The technique for making crown glass, perfected in the 14th century by French glassmakers in Normandy, was introduced into England in the 1560s, and crown glass was first produced commercially in this country by Henry Richards at the Bear Garden, Bankside, Southwark, c 1684.[21]

Before the Industrial Revolution, furnaces constructed to make glass were fuelled with charcoal. Silica was taken straight from rivers or quarried sand, with little regard for contaminants, and sands often contained metal oxides which discoloured the glass; beech wood ash, soda lime and other materials used in the smelting process also added colour to the glass, which was most commonly green or straw-coloured. This coloured glass was thick, relatively cheap and brittle, and helped protect plants from the fiercest heat of the sun, so that shading was not as necessary as it became after the introduction of colourless sheet glass. The colour of glass was improved in the early 19th century through the systematic application of crystallised soda, a process pioneered by the introduction of the Leblanc process for soda glass in the mid-1830s, when regular production of white glasses became increasingly common, as consistent materials became available, and more efficient coal and, later, gas-fired furnaces were introduced. Arsenic was often used as a decolouriser and refining agent from the 1830s until the 1870s.[22] The blinds at the Fernery in the Swiss Garden, outlined above, represented the need for new methods with which to minimise the effects of intense sunlight on plants in conservatories and glasshouses with the increasing use of white glass.

Revolutionary discoveries in the field of industrial chemistry, such as the process for making synthetic alkali, progressively found commercial application in the field of flat glass manufacture in Britain during the first half of the 19th century. The technology for producing and finishing glass was also refined with the invention of new products and processes, improved during a period of sustained experiment and commercial competition; the glazier/glass seller of the past was replaced by the specialist manufacturer. By 1826, London already boasted 14 such firms, and 10 years later that figure had increased to 32.[23] Until this time, the largest crown disc of glass produced by the most skilled glassworkers was approximately 1.5m in diameter, producing a maximum pane size of 0.6m square.[24]

The emergence of a novel breed of manufacturer is best exemplified by the development of three great early 19th-century British glassmaking concerns run respectively by the Chances (Stourbridge), James Hartley (Sunderland) and Pilkington-Greenhall (St Helens), entrepreneurs who, by 1851, had completely restructured the manufacture of glass. Lucas Chance marketed a new variety of German glass in 1838, and by 1845, when duties were eventually removed from glass, the manufacture of sheet glass became increasingly commonplace, as prices reduced dramatically. The new type of cylinder glass, known from the 1770s as 'German sheet glass', matched the earlier crown glass for colour and price without the limitation on the size of the glass sheet. Chance Bros Co Ltd won the contract for Paxton's giant glasshouse for the Great Exhibition of 1851 in Hyde Park, London, and between July 1850 and February 1851 approximately three million panes of 16oz sheet glass measuring 49 × 10 inches (over 956,000sq ft/88,815 sq m) were manufactured and installed, and that without interrupting the regular production schedule of the factory (see Fig 50).[25]

In around 1855, the 6th Duke of Devonshire extensively modernised the conservatory at Chiswick House, converting the sashes from small crown glass panes to larger panes of the 'best glass'. This produced two main benefits: the light entering the conservatory was increased both in quantity and quality, and the maintenance burden was reduced by the smaller number of glazing bars. Sometimes such conversion was made simply by cutting out intermediate glazing bars, as at Audley End, Essex, and Tatton Park, Cheshire, and reglazing with the larger sheets. The new glass that the 6th Duke installed in the conservatory at Chiswick may have been Hartley's Patent Rolled Plate, which was produced with finely combed grooves specifically for diffusing the sun's rays and thereby preventing scorching in conservatories (Fig 98).

Fig 98
A fragment of polished rolled plate recovered from the excavations at Chiswick, produced by imprinting the molten glass with a patterned roller. The grooves are at about 1.3mm centres and would have effectively diffused sunlight to prevent scorching of the plants. It may have been made by Hartleys in Sunderland or by Pilkington under licence. It is not possible to obtain a close match with modern glass. [McLaren, I 2005 *The Conservatory, Chiswick House, Burlington Lane, London: A Report on its History and Development 1812 to the Present Day* for English Heritage, p 59]

Glass of 21oz (per sq ft) was normally used for the roofs of conservatories and glasshouses, and 15oz glass was mostly used for vertical work, with average thicknesses of approximately 2.8mm and 2mm respectively. 'Wet glazing', introduced from Holland in the 1770s, using linseed putty was the norm, but some manufacturers preferred 'dry glazing', in which the glass was retained either by the incorporation of metal clips, channels and caps, or, in some instances, by folded lead T-sections, strips of lead which had the advantage of being available in very long continuous lengths. The advantage of the dry system was that panes could be replaced more easily.

The most common and attractive practice for glazing roofs was to use beaver-tailed panes laid with minimal lap. Established in the 1760s, the glass was cut with curved rather than straight upper and lower edges, encouraging the water to flow away from the wooden glazing bars towards the centre of the pane and increasing the rate at which rainwater was shed. Glazing conservatories and glasshouses with overlapping panes allowed more light to reach the plants, but the overlap eventually became discoloured, thereby reducing the light inside. Water also collected in the overlap, turning to ice when the temperature dropped below freezing, so that the panes were vulnerable to cracking by expanding ice. Curving the pane top and bottom so that water could collect naturally at the lowest part of the curve and drain away easily offered a partial solution to the problem. Putty was often used to seal the overlap, and the recommended width of the overlap was reduced from three-eighths of an inch (9.5mm) in the 1780s down to as little as one-eighth of an inch by the 1830s.

The combination of increased architectural endeavours in conservatory and glasshouse design in conjunction with requirements for new types of glass suitable for their designs, along with the removal of glass duty in 1845, enabled and promoted experimentation with cast plate glass production. Specific horticultural glass was manufactured in 1847, such as that used in the restoration of the conservatory at Chiswick House in the 1850s (*see* case study), which had a ribbed surface, diffusing the light and thereby reducing potential damage to vegetation.[26]

The narrow spacing of the wrought-iron glazing bars at Felton Park (Fig 99) is testament to its early construction date of *c* 1830, when the technologies for glass manufacture could only produce relatively small panes. It was, however, the use of small panes of glass that allowed the curve of the glasshouse roof to be so steep, as wider panes of such minimal depth would have been vulnerable to breakage. As Loudon had observed in his 1824 *Green-House Companion*, affirming that narrow panes of glass minimise the risk of damage from hail and frost:

> No slope of roof ... will guard against hail accompanied by wind: all that can be done ... is to adopt panes of glass of a small size and good quality – say not broader than seven inches and of Newcastle rather than Greenock manufacture. To guard against the breakage of glass by frost the panes should not overlap one another more than a quarter of an inch – as water will not lodge in the interstices between panes and consequently there being none to freeze there will be no panes broken.[27]

Fig 99
Fish-scale glazing to the greenhouse at Felton Park, Northumberland. [Spence and Dower Architects]

At Felton Park the glazing bars are spaced at exactly 7in (177.8mm) and the glass panes overlap only slightly more than Loudon's recommended quarter inch, the fish-scale edges to the upper and lower edges of each pane encouraging the water to drain down the centre of the glass, protecting the putty against the bars from wetting and icing up.

The trial project had indicated that it might be unnecessary to remove the glass panes of the roof unless they were found to be loose or cracked, a welcome discovery because of their function as a structural web between the wrought-iron glazing bars and concerns about the loss of historic glass during the removal process. Following initial brushing away of debris, loose fillet putty and dirt, all the glass panes were closely inspected to ascertain whether they were loose or cracked. Detailed schedules were prepared recording the status of each of the approximately 9,000 panes, all of which were also marked *in situ*, allowing sound, but loose, panes to be removed and later returned to their original place. Approximately 18 per cent of the panes were noted as broken, missing or in some way inappropriate, such as those to which repairs had been undertaken in square-cut panes, disrupting the fish-scale rhythm, along with other patterned, obscured glass considered unsuitable in the context.

As the trial project had demonstrated, it was necessary to remove the bottom two courses of panes from immediately above the cast-iron gutter in order to provide working access to the corroded ends of the wrought-iron glazing bars. It was noted that the narrow fish-scale courses of the curved section of the roof had survived in better condition than the longer panes of the shallow sloping roof above: more than a thousand larger panes had been lost from this zone and this had been an area of greater repair in the past.

All the new replacement glass was measured and cut on site. This proved essential because, although the glasshouse appeared to be absolutely regular, small discrepancies in the dimensions of spaces in between the glazing bars had to be noted to ensure a proper fit to the very narrow seat of the glazing bar. The panes were pressed into the back putty, but on the steeper front slope it was found that some tended to slip out of line before the putty could harden. This was overcome by fitting clothes-pegs over the feather of the bars to prevent slippage (Fig 100).

Fig 100
An economic method of providing temporary support against slippage of glass while the back putty is soft. [Spence and Dower Architects]

Glazing repair

The beauty of original handmade glass and its ability to reflect and disperse the light results from the method of manufacture. Original glass lends a particular aesthetic quality to any conservatory or glasshouse, and should be retained wherever possible. In situations where historic glass is partially missing, then very similar glass should be used to complement the original, although great care must be exercised in its choice, and specifications must be clear, never simply referring to 'cylinder' or 'crown' glass. There are several modern glasses available, such as cathedral glass, press-patterned glasses and machine-made 'antique' glasses, but placing them alongside handmade glass is generally unattractive and an indication of poor workmanship. Many modern handmade glasses commercially available today tend to be cylinder glass of one type or another. There are good imported glasses from Germany, France and Poland that are extremely close to old glasses that still survive, and it is these that must be sought out. There is now no handmade window glass made commercially in the UK.[28]

If frames are to be repaired, extracting original glass panes requires care and a considerable amount of time. Even once the face putty is removed, the thin line of putty between the glass and the frame often makes it impossible to remove the glass, in which case it is usually better to leave the glass in place, reface any lost or damaged putty with new, and refrain from disturbing surrounding framework if at all possible.

Where possible, glass should be inserted into a groove to produce a more durable junction (Fig 101). Where this is not possible, the panes should be laid on to putty in a rebate. Vertical work can be face-puttied, but it is not advisable to face-putty the roofs of conservatories and glasshouses because they are then more susceptible to the ingress of water from the top joint. The panes are best secured on their faces with either galvanised or non-ferrous glazing sprigs. These are effectively metal darts which, unlike pins, do not present line or point contact with the glass (Fig 102). They have the additional advantage that they do not part the grain to such an extent.

Fig 101 (opposite)
A diagram showing glass inserted into a groove. [Robert Jameson, Foster and Pearson]

Fig 102 (right)
Glass secured with non-ferrous glazing sprigs. [Robert Jameson, Foster and Pearson]

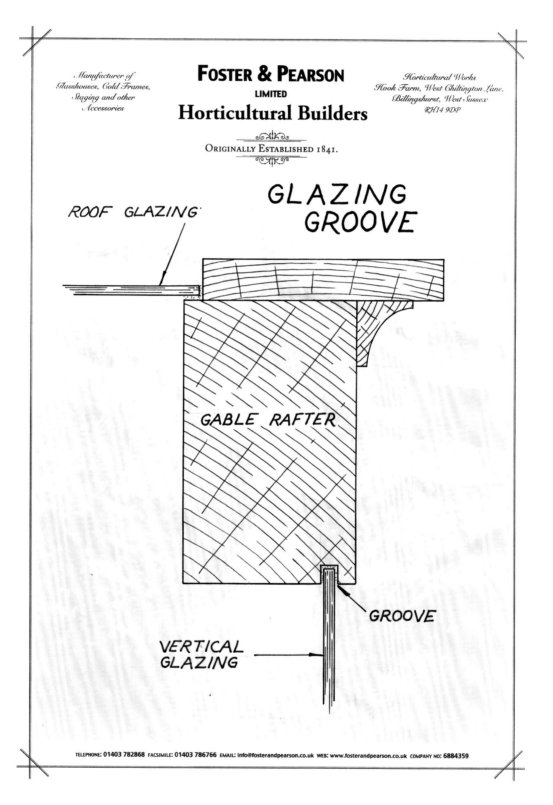

The conservatory at Came House (Fig 103) was restored between 1964 and 1967 by Donald Insall Associates architects.

Came House in Dorset was built by Francis Cartwright of Blandford in 1754 for the Damer family, and the conservatory, or winter garden, was added to the west side of the house, opening directly off the Morning Room, *c* 1840. On plan it is a rectangle, some 45ft (13.7m) long by 18ft (5.5m) wide, with an octagon approximately 27ft (8.2m) across at the centre, giving the effect of a nave and transepts. Above the octagon, raised on a vertical clerestory, soars an eight-sided glazed dome, supported on slender fluted columns enriched with acanthus leaf ornament. Similar curved and glazed roofs, comprising a delicate spider's web of cast-iron ribs with extremely light intermediate glazing bars, their rebates being barely one-eighth of an inch (3.2mm) in depth, cover the 'nave' and intersect with the central clerestory.

Fig 103

The conservatory at Came House, Dorset. [Donald Insall & Associates Architects]

When, in 1964, the owner, with the aid of a grant from the Historic Buildings Council, decided to restore the conservatory at Came, it was felt that the glazing framework was too damaged to be repainted and that curved glazing would be impossibly expensive and unable to be bedded in the very small rebates of the glazing bars. Most of the glazing to the segmental dome of the conservatory was broken and missing, having suffered years of weathering (Fig 104). Eventually, however, a start was made on descaling and repairing the rusted and corroded ironwork, the work being undertaken by a local blacksmith, E G Carnell & Son.

The owner was strongly in favour of using acrylic sheet as a reglazing material and, after much discussion and research, this was agreed, the material being considered to have several advantages: it could be cut accurately to size, was completely transparent and could be bent cold to a curve on site. The acrylic sheet was bonded to the metalwork, which was coated with a metal primer, using a special double adhesive. A trial of the 'reglazing' of a few bays was undertaken through the winter months, and proved to be successful. Thus encouraged, the whole of the roof was tackled by a small, but dedicated, team of craftsmen. The work proved difficult: no two ribs were equally spaced, so each section of sheet 'glazing' had to be cut to its own template with a special electric saw, and some of the frame members were perished and had to be replaced. When the entire roof had been filled in with acrylic sheet, a protective sheathing, consisting of a strip of high-grade aluminium backed with a bitumen-based adhesive, was applied over the exterior of the ribs and glazing bars, overlapping the edges of the sheets. The restoration works to the conservatory were completed in July 1967.

Fig 104
The dilapidated dome of the
conservatory prior to restoration
work. [Donald Insall & Associates
Architects]

One of the most interesting and challenging aspects of this project was the reglazing work to the cast-iron roof. While dismantling was relatively straightforward because there was so little glass remaining, reglazing was very exacting. The rebates on both the main cast-iron ribs and the copper glazing bars (Fig 105) are barely 2mm wide, and this was one of the reasons why all of the salvaged glass was grouped together. Each roof segment was subdivided into seven sections by moulded glazing bars barely 25mm deep by 13mm wide. These were secured in alignment by iron saddle bars (two per segment/subdivision) which spanned between the main ribs at roughly equal distances and were secured with bespoke copper clips soldered to the underside of the glazing bars (Fig 106). Glass quarries were installed in each subdivision and brought up at the same level. Only when the glass reached the level of the saddle bar would copper wires – most of the clips incapable of being reused because they had snapped, seized or become brittle – be secured by twisting them around the saddle bars, the glass and glazing bars below becoming relatively rigid.

As the curve of the roof began to flatten out, the scaffolding had to be adjusted several times in order to enable the glaziers to lie over the finished work to continue to the top; how the original builders and glaziers managed is not known. While traditional linseed oil putty was used originally, it was agreed that a modern glazing compound, a rubber butyl linseed oil putty with good elasticity, would best cope with the extremes of temperature and remain weatherproof. It was accepted, however, that a constant lap between glass tiles may result in water being blown under the glass close to the top of the roof during storm conditions. The replacement glass was Polish cylinder glass.

Fig 105

Narrow rebates to glazing bars.

[© Historic England/John Tiernan]

Fig 106

Bespoke copper clips soldered to the underside of the glazing bars. [© Historic England/ John Tiernan]

The majority of the Fernery in the Swiss Garden had been glazed with modern float glass in the early 21st century, although a minimal amount of cylinder glass had survived. Following the application to the ironwork of a two-pack epoxy primer and inter-coat, the glasshouse was reglazed using over 4,800 hand-cut panes of 3mm cylinder sheet glass (broad glass),[29] cut with side clearance in order to prevent damage from the upstands of the glazing bars, bedded and faced-up with a paint-compatible, modified polymer sealant that could be profiled to mimic linseed oil putty.[30] The overlap between the heads and tails of the panes was 20–22mm.

SYON PARK, LONDON

The glazing in the dome of the Great Conservatory at Syon Park, a commercial horticultural float glass installed during the 1980s refurbishment and pointed into the cast-iron ribs using silicone, was deteriorating in parts, allowing rainwater to enter the conservatory. The existing float glass did not achieve the level of protection required, and was replaced using a vertical machine-drawn glass, which can be toughened but also imparts a slightly irregular appearance to the glazing, considered more appropriate to the style of the conservatory building than a completely flat glass. The glass is manufactured in Germany by Schott Glass under the name of Goetheglas and processed and distributed by Pearsons Glazing of Liverpool. A full scaffold was erected inside and outside the building to facilitate the repairs. The existing glass was removed by knifing out the old silicone pointing. The old bedding materials were then removed back to a sound substrate, which involved removal of most of the paint layers on the glazing bars to provide a suitable surface for redecoration. The extended order period required for the glazing meant that it had to be ordered before full scaffold access was available. This was achieved using mobile access towers. The major problem encountered was difficulty in installing the glass into the curved sections, where the increased thickness of the toughened glass had in some places increased the gaps between overlapping panes. Some additional cutting was required to overcome this problem.

Woodwork

Straight-grained Scandinavian red deal, a softwood, was the most commonly used timber for conservatory and glasshouse work during the 19th century because of its inherent stability and durability; it also tends to receive paint more readily than most hardwoods. However, the increasing availability of Burmese teak in the mid-1880s meant this could be used for the finest work or where additional durability was required, for example, in the tropical conditions found in orchid and other hothouses.

Timber maintenance

New timber decays much more readily than that used up to around the middle of the 20th century. Until around this time, timber was taken from virgin forest where – unlike modern plantation-grown timber, where quantity rather than quality may, arguably, be said to be the driving force – it grew slowly, producing a tighter-grained and more resinous, and therefore more durable, product. This was generically termed 'pitch pine'.[31] Because there are virtually no virgin forests left in Scandinavia, Douglas fir, which was not readily available in the 19th century, is now substituted, and is, effectively, a more appropriate product because it can be obtained in very long, clear, close-grained lengths. Burmese teak was used in tropical houses, such as those at the Chelsea Physic Garden, and although it is still available, for reasons of sustainability its use is rather frowned upon, and it is extremely expensive. Smooth-grained iroko is an excellent alternative.

Surprisingly, small sections of timber (Fig 107) proved to be more durable than larger sections in the generally humid conditions of conservatories and glasshouses, as deeper sections retain more moisture, making them prone to decay. Wet and dry rot and beetle infestation are the most common form of biological attack. Ensuring that the environment is low in moisture and humidity, and that the conditions are light, well ventilated and clean, prevents infestation. Dry rot

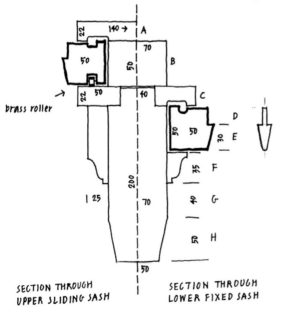

SECTION THROUGH
UPPER SLIDING SASH

SECTION THROUGH
LOWER FIXED SASH

Fig 107

A survey drawing of a typical early 19th-century glasshouse rafter carrying a sliding sash on each side; the upper sash ran on small brass rollers over the lower fixed sash, which would be detachable for maintenance. The running sash would be held on counterweights, rather like a sash window, but sometimes they would run on a rack and pinion track operated by a ground-level winding mechanism, a method that was used at Holkham Hall in Norfolk. The rafter was often built up with small sections like this to create a weatherproof junction between the sashes and the rafter, but it would not be resistant to violent storms. The capping piece (A) stopped as soon as it was clear of the upper running sash. The original Chiswick House conservatory roof may have been similar to this one. [McLaren, I 2005 *The Conservatory, Chiswick House, Burlington Lane, London: A Report on its History and Development 1812 to the Present Day* for English Heritage] requires moisture contents in excess of 28 per cent, but once established the fungi can remain active at moisture contents of more than 20 per cent, and it can remain dormant at still lower levels. More problematically, dry rot can transport moisture from the source, enabling it to colonise dry timber further afield, often travelling between the masonry plinth and the timber above. This makes eradication very difficult in conservatories and glasshouses, and the removal of some timbers may be required. Timber should therefore be kept clean and well protected.

It is best to take paintwork right back to the timber if using modern paints, because they do not always adhere to old paint types, however well prepared they might be. Care must be taken to use adequate protection when removing lead-based paints, which were commonplace until the 1960s.

Whereas existing timbers in building elements which do not have a structural function, such as sash windows, can be reused, existing timbers in conservatories and glasshouses that have deteriorated through lack of maintenance have often lost their inherent structural qualities, rendering them unsuitable for reuse in conservation. If splicing or repairing timber, always try to obtain a good fit and use an appropriate glue together with non-ferrous fixings.

HILTON PARK, STAFFORDSHIRE

Fig 108 (below)
Timber ribs rebated and capped with a narrow timber strip.
[© Historic England/John Tiernan]

Fig 109 (below right)
The glazed dome was completely rebuilt using Sapele, as opposed to good-quality softwood, as its durability would be greater in a potentially damp environment. This illustration shows the primary timber ribs for the glazing under construction.
[© Historic England/John Tiernan]

The joinery used to construct the north-west side of the glazed roof at Hilton Park is comparable in its inventiveness with laminations of straight-grained timber glued and screwed together to form primary and secondary ribs of slender cross-section spanning maximum distances. Where the metal ribs were cast with narrow rebates to hold the glass with putty, those made from timber were simply rebated and capped with a narrow timber strip (Figs 108 and 109). Because of its dilapidated condition, it was difficult to ascertain whether the roof timbers were primary fabric.

The very nature of this type of building required thinking about maintenance at the outset and while 'repair as found' was the guiding mantra, making incremental changes to ensure that maintenance was kept to a minimum was always to the fore. The timber roof had to be completely rebuilt and, as it was painted, it was agreed after discussion that sapele hardwood could be used, as opposed to good-quality softwood, because its durability would be greater in a potentially damp environment.

Surface coatings

Preparation

Surface coatings and preparation of metal and timber are, arguably, the most important aspects in the conservation of conservatories and glasshouses. Surface preparation aims to provide a physically and chemically stable surface with a micro-profile suitable for adhesion of the priming coat, one of the most important factors determining the long-term success of the surface coatings. Surfaces must be free of loose material, grease and oils, which can be removed by degreasing compounds, solvents or steam-cleaning if necessary. Great care must be taken in the removal of rust and, if it is deemed appropriate, existing paintwork, in order not to damage surface detail, decoration, tooling marks, arises and edges. Traditional cast iron usually carries a thin burnt-on foundry skin which is protective and should not be removed. Similarly, mill scale is often found on wrought iron, and must not be removed if it is still adhering. The least intrusive method of cleaning should be selected in order to achieve a stable, clean surface.

One mechanical process to remove extraneous material from ironwork is dry abrasive cleaning, such as the selective and careful use of grit blasting, which may be used to remove paint and rust from cast iron, although there are risks attached to the method, not least of which is damage to the protective skin formed during the casting or forging process. It is essential to select a grit suitable specifically for cast iron. In a workshop environment, chilled iron shot can be filtered and recycled.

The dry abrasive process is fast, effective and widely available, but potentially hazardous, both to personnel and adjoining materials. Trials should always be undertaken to establish non-damaging levels of air pressure, grit size and hardness. On wrought iron low pressure and fine grit can be used, although, ideally, wrought iron should not be grit blasted because the process can remove the protective layer of mill scale formed during its manufacture.

Wet abrasive cleaning is similar to dry abrasive cleaning, but a water/abrasive slurry is used. In this process soluble salts and corrosion can be washed out of crevices, but wet ironwork rusts quickly, and there is a risk of water being forced into joints and porous castings. Specialised systems, such as JOS vortex blasting, are available for applications requiring close control, like the removal of individual layers of paint, and for use on soft metals. Washing should be continued until all salts are removed, and a primer should be applied once surfaces are dry and before visible re-rusting (gingering) occurs. Ultra-high-pressure water-jetting, using water at pressures up to 800 bar, may be used to remove rust and paint without abrasives. Metalwork in polluted or coastal environments should be spray-washed at pressures up to 200 bar, with clean water containing a maximum concentration of 0.2% corrosion inhibitor to remove salts.

An advantage of wet abrasive cleaning is that airborne dust is reduced, which may be appropriate where the structure has to be blasted *in situ*, particularly relevant in urban contexts. The process requires specialist operator training. It is also potentially hazardous to personnel and adjoining materials.

Another method employed to burn off paint and spall away rust is flame cleaning, in which an oxygen-propane flame is passed over the surface of the metal. Being non-abrasive, this is particularly suitable for the soft surface of wrought iron, and is effective in dislodging rust packed behind scrolls, waterleaves and other decorative ornamentation.

Where necessary, paint can also be removed from ironwork using chemicals. These can be applied in the form of a gel or poultice to soften paint, which can then be scraped and washed off. Chemical products often contain toxic and/or corrosive chemicals which must be treated with care and appropriate precautions should be employed. Smaller items may be pickled in acid to remove rust and paint. The porosity of cast iron and traps in wrought ironwork render them open to contamination from the blasting medium and chemicals. Steps should be taken to prevent this by using only an abrasive medium for cast iron and by ensuring that chemically cleaned metalwork is thoroughly washed after cleaning. There are other methods of mechanically cleaning, such as wire-brushing, needle-gunning and the use of descaling chisels, although none really compare to grit-blasting.

Bare patches on ironwork can be rubbed back with abrasive cloth, primed, undercoated and again rubbed back to blend, before final finish-coating. On thick coats, damaged areas can be brought forward with a filler, such as red-lead putty or polyester resin, after priming. The chalky, powdery surface of lead paints provides a poor substrate, but can sometimes be recoated with linseed, alkyd oil paint or paints formulated for use on ferrous metal, after rubbing back. Trial areas, left to weather, should be carried out to verify the level of adhesion. Many early paints contain lead, which is toxic and cumulative in the body, so cleaning methods must be chosen to minimise dispersal and loss of toxic material, and appropriate personal protective equipment used. Where lead paints are removed, their debris, together with spent abrasives and other extraneous materials, must be transferred to a certified waste-management contractor.

Priming and colours

From antiquity, ironwork has been treated for protection and decorated. Internally, architectural metalwork was often finished by painting, surface-colouring, and later, by plating. Externally, protection was paramount, so painting was usual, or, from the late-19th century, cathodic metal coating. As well as lead-based oil paints, lacquers, varnishes and waxes have all been found on wrought ironwork, and bitumen paints were also sometimes used.

Traditionally, the simplest form of decoration to metalwork was colouring of the surface itself by heating and dipping it in various liquids to create a range of colours, principally dark blues or light/dark browns. This process was cosmetic rather than protective, however, so was generally used for indoor metalwork only.

Colours for metalwork were originally produced by crushing and blending natural pigments – such as raw or burnt-earth colours, like ochres, umbers and siennas – into a suitable medium and mixing them with a binder. Linseed oil, made by crushing flax, and used since the

11th century, is the most common traditional binder. It has a light-yellow tint, and dries by absorption of oxygen (oxidation) over several days. Its drying time was reduced to about one day by boiling, or by adding a 'dryer' such as lead, manganese or cobalt. In order to reduce the risk of skinning and cracking, extenders, including chalk and mica, were added to bulk up the paint and form a paste which was easier to apply and covered arises more effectively. Thinners were mixed with the binder to change its working properties and vary the final level of gloss; more thinners in the final coat gave a higher gloss. Turpentine, distilled from pine-tree sap, was the most common traditional thinner, until 1885 when the synthetic 'turps' substitute, or white spirit, became available.

One of the most common coatings for ironwork was white lead (lead carbonate), produced by the enforced corrosion of lead sheets by acetic acid (vinegar). Less stable colours were obtained from vegetable and animal sources such as plants, berries, logwood and even, as in the case of cochineal red, the dried bodies of a South American cactus beetle. Black was obtained from soot or lampblack, but was not commonly used on outdoor metalwork until the advent of alkyd oil paints in the 1930s. Many pigments would not mix easily with binders, so grinding and incorporating was undertaken by specialised paint makers, and paints were blended and sold by 'colourmen'.

All the above-mentioned pigments have been used on indoor metalwork, but white lead, providing white, and a white base for other colours, was most commonly used on the exterior of structures for priming and finishing of both timber and metalwork. Added pigments produced creams, 'stone' colours (sometimes tinted to blend with adjacent wall surfaces) and greys, including 'lead' colour. 'Anti-corrosion' and 'lithic' paints may have included crushed glass, scoria from leadworks, burnt oyster shells and various natural minerals. Paints containing white lead may now only be used on Grade I and II* listed buildings after authorisation from Historic England.

Other finishes to metalwork traditionally included red lead, or minium orange (lead tetroxide), widely used in the Middle Ages for the decoration of manuscripts and painting. Often boiled with linseed oil to improve drying properties, it was used from antiquity as a primer, along with red oxide, a cheap, hard-wearing paint. Finishing colours included 'invisible', or Brunswick, green, the first synthetic colour, and bronze greens, a range of greens often used in garden settings, made by mixing lemon chrome, Prussian blue and trace pigments. Smalt (cobalt glass blue) and other rare and costly pigments were occasionally used by the wealthy for prestige metalwork on prominent façades from the 18th century. Paint with rare pigments must be conserved if found and not overcoated.

Gloss finish on metalwork, achieved with varnish, was not uncommon, but lead-based paints soon weathered to a matt/chalky surface. Varnish, clear pale-yellow resinous lacquer, was used as a gloss finish coat, and coal tar and natural bitumen were often mixed with solvents for use as thick protective coatings in functional applications. Gilding was commonly applied to decoration on fine ornamental ironwork.[32]

Metal components at Hilton Park were cleaned by dry abrasive blasting using aluminium oxide particles – a relatively soft abrasive – at low pressure, following trials by the metalwork subcontractor. This process was employed in order to achieve a cleaned surface with suitable roughness to facilitate good paint adhesion, while ensuring that the original protective foundry scale was not eroded.

Lead-based paints were originally used as finishes to the conservatory at Hilton Park, but a modern synthetic paint of proven durability was chosen to replace them. A two-part epoxy-based paint was chosen for the metalwork, as this would provide surface protection to the metal for 20–25 years. A combination of brush and spray application was used.

Due to the condition of the metalwork, paint analysis had not been a primary consideration at the outset because no surface coating appeared to have survived, but, through redistribution of some of the project development investigation funds, James Finlay,[33] a historic paint consultant, was commissioned to carry out investigation work. This identified previous paint schemes, which were then used to inform decision-making.

Modern finishes

Conservatories and glasshouses heat up very quickly in the morning sunlight and moisture from micro-porous paints, which act as a barrier to liquid water but allow water vapour to pass through, cannot be expelled through the paint quickly enough, resulting in blistering. Linseed oil paints offer satisfactory alternatives to modern systems, and modern hand-applied paints are capable of giving a service life in excess of ten years.

Paints cure to a dry film ranging in thickness from a few microns for a thin traditional paint, to over 100 microns per coat for modern high-build coatings. The film's thickness and uniformity depends on the paint's formulation and viscosity, the method of application and the skill of the painter. Because the wet film tends to recede from arises, and thicken in crevices, it is necessary to apply several coats, normally at least three. A minimum dry film thickness of 250 microns is recommended on outdoor metalwork.

In the 20th century, linseed oil paints have been replaced by petrochemical-based resins with synthetic pigments. The first, dating from the 1920s, were alkyd resins, which were stronger, tougher and faster-drying than linseed oil, and provided intense white (using titanium oxide pigment) and black, both of which became common on metalwork and are still used widely today. Provided traditional oil-based paint coats have dried fully and are adhering well, they can be overcoatable with a modern single-pack water-based system. Alkyd systems should be trialled well in advance to check for the substrate's susceptibility to solvent attack, and allowed to weather in order to check adhesion.

Primers, often rich in zinc or aluminium to provide cathodic protection, wet the metal surface and provide adhesion for subsequent coats. Intermediate coats provide thickness, opacity and colour, and finishing coats provide colour, texture and first defence against the environment. Coatings must be compatible with one another and, for this reason, manufacturers have devoted considerable resources to developing complete paint systems for specific applications, for which their guidance should be sought. They will, of course, only guarantee their products if they are applied in accordance with their own instructions.

Paint application

Traditionally, paint was thinned and applied by animal hair or bristle brushes. The skill of the painter was paramount in achieving a coat of full coverage, uniform thickness and good final appearance. While modern paints contain additives to ease the transfer of paint from brush to workpiece, spreading and curing, and are applied to tightly defined specifications, the skill and integrity of the painter remain critical. The advantages of brush application are that minimal equipment is required and a good coverage can be achieved on difficult profiles, but its disadvantages are that it is a relatively slow process and the individual coats tend to be rather thin. Rollers are faster, but really only suitable for applying modern paints to large flat surfaces. Conventional spray techniques require more coats but are relatively fast, especially on complex shapes. However, spraying may produce poor adhesion to timber compared with hand-brushing, where paint can be worked into the grain.[34]

THE SWISS GARDEN, BEDFORDSHIRE

The importance of the ironwork in the Fernery at the Swiss Garden in Bedfordshire prompted the specification of paints that would reduce further maintenance demands as well as provide a high degree of protection. This meant removal of the mainly modern glass (extensive survival of historic glass would have necessitated a different approach) to ensure that surface coatings would extend into rebates, and stripping back to bare metal, historic paint analysis having established that, other than tiny fragments, no historic decorative scheme had survived.

Following removal of early 20th-century glass, the ironwork of the Grotto and Fernery at the Swiss Garden was cleaned on site using ultra-high-pressure water jet cleaning, an environmentally friendly system that would achieve a degree of cleaning more effective, and less intrusive, than abrasive cleaning methods, such as blasting with copper slag. The method used applied water to the surface of the metal at a pressure of approximately 40,000psi or 275MPa, attaining a cleaning standard of Wa2.5, the high-pressure water jetting equivalent of the Sa2.5 abrasive standard.[35] Adjacent materials, landscape and planting were protected to prevent damage from over-blast, and provision had to be made for safely catching and collecting arisings, which may have contained lead-based paints.

The view was taken that, given that conservation of ironwork is heavily dependent on coatings, traditional paints would be eschewed and a modern paint system would be used that could provide the highest degree of protection for the longest possible time. This meant the use of an advanced modern paint system comprising two-pack epoxy and polyurethane paint in mid-blue, identified by the paint analysis as close to the original colour, brush-applied with a traditional flat (sheen) finish.

Historic paint analysis was undertaken by Dr Brian Singer of Northumbria University, although only small patches of paint in interior internal angles provided adequate data for the preparation of cross-sectional analysis. Because there was so little evidence of historic paints on the ironwork at Felton Park, once the loose and cracked glass had been removed, the exposed ironwork was cleaned using hand tools and rotating steel brushes in order to remove old encrusted putty and small patches of paint, as well as burnishing off surface rust inside and outside the frame.

A trial project was undertaken by Calibre Metalwork and modern paints were selected for finishing. A liquid rust converter,[36] was applied, forming, in conjunction with a butoxyethanol solvent wetting agent, a protective chemical barrier on the ironwork. This was an extremely useful process for penetrating the gaps beneath the overlapping panes, where the reaction with small pockets of inaccessible rust could neutralise further corrosion. The process was followed by a primer and two-coat Alkathane paint system.[37]

General maintenance and conservation guidelines

- Periodic inspection should be carried out by competent persons, and comprehensive written maintenance schedules and operation guidelines generated where appropriate.

- Maintaining good drainage and weathering is essential. Care should be taken to ensure that brickwork, copings and lead flashings are kept in good order, and that gutters, hopperheads and drainage pipes are running freely, through regular clearance of biological growth and debris.

- Maintenance priorities must be to keep any joints sealed and maintain paintwork, which, ideally, should be rubbed down and touched up every two years, renewing defective putties.

- Glass should be kept clean and free from lichen and mould, and putty work should be regularly inspected; microcracks in glass allow dirt to settle.

- Maintenance and operational staff should be selected for their skill and diligence and provided with appropriate training.

- Budgets for planned short- and medium-term maintenance should be provided.

New conservatories

Technical developments in the types of materials used for the construction of glass structures today, and experience of the behaviour of earlier conservatories and glasshouses, provide contemporary architects with a fund of knowledge and possibilities unavailable to their forebears in the 18th and 19th centuries. Choice of material for both new construction and conservation is generally dependent upon market availability, although subject to innovation, as in the case of Loudon's small-scale, wrought-iron glazing bar.

But innovative technologies must be approached with extreme caution: the use of untested materials can have devastating consequences when employed in the conservation of historic structures. Traditional materials and techniques, increasingly available today in the wake of concerted efforts to preserve and restore historic structures during the latter part of the last century, have proved the most efficacious in the conservation of historic conservatories and glasshouses.

Even materials that were deemed appropriate during the last 50 years have been shown to be unsuitable for both conservation and new work for these specialist structures with their very particular requirements for construction and environmental control. Aluminium, for example, increasingly used for new conservatories in the second half of the 20th century, is subject to flexing, and sections used in the construction of modern aluminium conservatories and glasshouses frequently fail as a result of metal fatigue, caused by work-hardening due to the flexing. Unlike aluminium, timber is not vulnerable to this deterioration because it does not tire from flexing and has the additional benefit of reducing condensation.

But increasingly rigorous testing and regulatory standards mean that new materials can now be engaged with increasing confidence. Advances in glass production, for example, provide more possibilities to echo the delicate glazing bars of the 18th century more closely than ever before, and modern environmental technologies allow humidity and environmental control to be monitored with increasing ease. The following case studies offer three very different approaches to the design and construction of these culturally and socially enduring structures in the 21st century.

Hugh Petter from ADAM Architecture won a limited RIBA competition in 2006 for the refurbishment of a Grade II listed Georgian townhouse, together with a new conservatory building (Fig 110) containing a swimming pool, gymnasium, changing rooms and ancillary areas.

 The effect of the conservatory on the setting of the listed townhouse was an important consideration, and the need to maintain views from the house to the bottom of the garden, some eighty metres away, was considered significant. The conservatory was therefore sited on the south side of the garden, behind the former coach house, an ideal location because the building was close enough to the main house to allow access through a new covered 'link' building, and the view of the garden from the house was retained. The covered link from the main house to the conservatory provided an opportunity to restore the Regency-inspired cast-iron veranda that dominates the back of the house. The area under the veranda at lower ground-floor level provided the first section of the link and was carefully enclosed with green metal-framed single glazing. The second half of the link was a more conventional structure, decorated with an entablature and pilasters in painted timber.

 The conservatory was conceived as a simple garden structure, the Tuscan order – the 'solidest and least ornate' of the orders – being chosen to articulate the Portland stone garden façade that breaks forward towards the garden. The other walls are built with London stock brick in lime mortar, with arched

Fig 110

A new conservatory in South London viewed from the garden. [ADAM Architecture]

121

window openings below rubbed brick arches, while the Portland stone cornice of the garden façade continues around the building to provide a harmonious continuity. A large roof light was placed above the centre of the swimming pool and glazed timber double doors open directly on to a terrace of Yorkstone paving, in front of a large lawn. Because of its visibility from the upper parts of the house, the roof of the conservatory was designed as the 'fifth elevation', and was clad with lead sheet, punctuated by the roof light over the pool.

The conservatory doors were glazed with slim toughened double glazing (4mm glass, 6mm cavity, 4mm glass), which requires a smaller rebate in the glazing bar than standard double glazing. This meant that the conservatory glazing bars were a similar thickness to the glazing bars of the single-glazed windows of the main house. The large roof light above the conservatory was constructed in aluminium-framed standard toughened double glazing due to the large pane sizes and the need to provide a robust and low-maintenance structure. The house and conservatory were partly heated by a ground source heat pump that was linked to a supply water borehole at the bottom of the garden. The waste water was returned to a discharge borehole nearer the house.

Tradition, of course, does not require an absence of technology: the swimming pool has a movable floor that can be raised to the surrounding floor level to allow the conservatory to be used in its more conventional sense.

One particular issue, which is fairly common for garden buildings, was the effect of a tree root protection area (RPA) on the siting of the conservatory. As a rule of thumb, the RPA radius from the centre of a tree is the stem diameter multiplied by 12. The two mature trees in question were on the far side of an old brick wall, and an experienced arboriculturalist advised that the RPA would in this case be offset because the roots would generally not find their way below the wall's foundation. Planning permission was subsequently granted on the basis that the excavation next to the conservatory side of the wall should be hand dug (Fig 111).

Fig 111
A view of the conservatory with
the Georgian townhouse behind.
[ADAM Architecture]

As part of the re-presentation work to Whitstable Castle, Martin Ashley Architects were asked in 2006 to replace a utilitarian extension with a new conservatory (Fig 112), which would enhance the rest of the building and provide a new facility which could be accessed from the new garden terrace to the west and from the main drive to the east. The conservatory had to reuse the existing footprint of the previous structure and incorporate the existing basement plant room below.

Whitstable Castle is situated on the ridge between Whitstable and Tankerton, overlooking the harbour. The earliest part of the castle, the octagonal tower and house, was built by Charles Pearson in 1790, and was then known as The Manor House. By 1836 it was sold to Wynn Ellis who extended it in 1840 to become Tankerton Tower, and used it as a summer residence. The last phase of major construction occurred in the 1920s when Albert Mallandain enlarged the building to the north of the octagonal tower and added a conservatory to the south; this was rebuilt during 1960s with a flat-roofed system building.

The new conservatory was required to replace the utilitarian 1960s extension, considered a detraction from the romantic style of the earlier castle building; it was designed in the spirit of the 18th- and 19th-century building, with similar features such as castellations, ornamental round turrets, canted end bay and Gothick arched doors and windows. Portland stone dressings were used for door and window surrounds, together with hood mouldings and castellated merlons to the parapet. Kent ragstone and flint walling was separated by bands of Portland stone, and the new turrets concealed the flues from the basement boiler room. On the south side, the canted end integrates the building into the new landscape design. The large double-glazed roof was inset into a traditional lead roof with parapet gutters, enhancing the view from the overlooking windows of the room above.

Internally (Fig 113), the conservatory is articulated with decorative arches and pilasters in fibrous plaster, based on existing examples within the building, with ashlar lining to the walls. The existing openings into the ground floor of the

Fig 112

Whitstable Castle, with the new garden room/conservatory to the right. [Martin Ashley Architects]

castle were altered to provide one large opening with timber-panelled reveals and French doors. The conservatory floor is paved with limestone tiles over new underfloor heating.

External areas directly abutting the building were altered to improve ambulant disabled access, to suit new and reinstated entrances in a manner so as to accord with and enhance the historic whimsical character of this folly building. On the west garden side, the existing terrace was raised to provide outdoor seating to the conservatory and to form a setting for larger functions. On the east side, the ground levels were re-laid to suit the new disabled entrance door, with a bridge over the new stone steps to the basement plant room. New planted areas were enclosed by flint and stone dwarf retaining walls.

Fig 113
The new, double-glazed roof enhances the view from the windows of the castle, and the interior is articulated with decorative arches and pilasters based on existing examples within the castle. [Martin Ashley Architects]

In 2009, the London-based architect Chris Dyson was asked to restore an early 18th-century former merchant's house in Whites Row, Spitalfields, London (Fig 114). The house had been badly neglected during its previous use as offices, clearly lacking the care and attention of a residential occupant, and poor planning decisions had blighted the rear aspect of the property, causing the garden at the lower-floor level to feel overshadowed and forlorn.

Situated in the former Tenter Ground Estate, this fine merchant's house was built between 1724 and 1743. The house is double-fronted, containing a semi-basement, three storeys and a roof garret. The plan is simple, with a staircase compartment between two rooms of equal size, each with a small closet projecting at the back (Fig 115). The aim externally was to strip away white

Fig 114

The front elevation of the former merchant's house in Whites Row, Spitalfields, London. [Chris Dyson Architect]

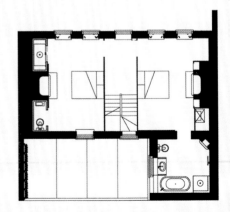

Fig 115

The second-floor plan. [Chris Dyson Architect]

paint to the brick frontage, repair and restore the masonry and timber windows, and place pleached limes and yew to the front area, bringing greenery to the street and increasing the domestic privacy of the house.

The rear aspect was dismal, and it was proposed to improve this through the addition of a green wall on the east-facing rear party wall, disguising a blank, unfashionable, 1980s brick elevation and providing greenery on all sides of the wall, thus giving improved views both into and out of the house. In the semi-basement, light now floods into the newly glazed courtyard, bringing air into the lower levels of the house, which had previously been dark, dank and depressing (Fig 116).

Early on in the design process it was decided to make a grand conservatory, two storeys in height, that would create a significant focus for family life in the house, replacing the absence of a garden and its associated amenities.

Four pieces of glass, two of which are fixed and two retractable, allow the dining room to be exposed to the elements on brighter days and enclosed when required. This, in turn, is complemented by a huge green wall, both inside and out of the glazing, drawing the eye up towards the sky. The success of this modern conservatory lies in the simplicity and elegance of the all-glass architectural detailing (Fig 117).

Historic England and the conservation department at the London Borough of Tower Hamlets were very supportive of the approach to restore this fine merchant's house, and restoration has inspired a new square opposite, within the former fruit and wool exchange redevelopment. This is an excellent example of how conservation of heritage assets, and care and attention to architectural fabric, can inspire modern redevelopment.

Fig 116 (below)
The interior of the new glazed courtyard. [Chris Dyson Architect]

Fig 117 (below right)
The interior of the new glazed courtyard. [Peter Landers]

Notes

1   Louw 1991.
2   During the First World War, Foster and Pearson lost most of their workforce, after which there was less demand for conservatories in Britain. Following the Second World War, the company continued as a producer of boilers and heating components until its demise in 2009, when the company was re-established by Robert Jameson, an agricultural engineer and expert in rural estate management. Foster and Pearson now restore and manufacture new conservatories and glasshouses strictly to the company's original design, as well as those of other manufacturers, including Messenger & Co, Boulton and Paul, Mackenzie and Moncur, Richardsons, Duncan Tucker, and so on. A fire destroyed all the original Foster and Pearson records at the end of the 20th century, but, through painstaking research, the new company has assembled a portfolio of their original customers, as well as those of other companies. Robert Jameson has compiled a library of profiles and methods of construction, in addition to a very considerable number of patterns of both Foster and Pearson's and other companies' 19th-century conservatories and glasshouses, which enables the newly formed company to reproduce the iron components to their original form.
3   The authors are grateful to Geoff Wallis CEng MIMechE, Dorothea Restorations, and Robert Jameson, Foster and Pearson Ltd, for advice, consultation and notes for the information contained in this section.
4   The authors are grateful to Geoff Wallis CEng MIMechE,

Dorothea Restorations, for advice, consultation and notes for the information contained in this section.
5   *App ASPC Scotland* 1814, p 453.
6   Repton 1805, pp 105–6. The conservatory was never erected.
7   Repton 1805, p 106.
8   Eaton Hodgkinson (1789–1861) had demonstrated in the 1830s that cast iron's strength in compression is about five times its strength in tension.
9   The authors are grateful to Geoff Wallis CEng MIMechE, Dorothea Restorations, and Robert Jameson, Foster and Pearson Ltd, for advice, consultation and notes for the information contained in this section.
10 Henry Bessemer invented the Bessemer converter, which enabled steel to be produced more economically than before, in 1856.
11 Loudon 1818, p 314.
12 The authors are grateful to Geoff Wallis CEng MIMechE, Dorothea Restorations, and Robert Jameson, Foster and Pearson Ltd, for advice, consultation and notes for the information contained in this section.
13 Grundy *et al* 1999, p 281.
14 Loudon 1833, pp 980–81.
15 McIntosh 1838, p 234.
16 The authors are grateful to Geoff Wallis CEng MIMechE, Dorothea Restorations, for advice, consultation and notes for the information contained in this section.
17 See list of potential consultants and suppliers.
18 As a ferrous metal corrodes it expands, such that fully developed rust can occupy seven times the volume of the original metal.

19 Centring, or centres, are curved temporary timber supports, generally used to form or build an arch.
20 The only grant for the project came from Historic England, with the grantee paying the balance. This was a standard Heritage at Risk (two stage) Development and Repair Grant: a development grant was offered that covered all the investigation works and professional fees; an in-principle repair grant was offered at the same time, which was confirmed when the tender costs were known at the end of the project development stage. The grant given covered approximately 80 per cent of the total cost of the project.
21 Louw 1991, p 48.
22 Castagnino 2013, p 8.
23 Louw 1991, p 48.
24 Castagnino 2013, p 1.
25 Louw 1991, p 58.
26 Castagnino 2013, p 1.
27 Loudon 1825, p 21.
28 See list of potential consultants and suppliers.
29 See list of potential consultants and suppliers.
30 See list of potential consultants and suppliers.
31 Analysis has shown that timber used by Foster and Pearson in 19th-century conservatories and glasshouses originated from northern Finland (Robert Jameson, Foster and Pearson).
32 The authors are grateful to Geoff Wallis CEng MIMechE, Dorothea Restorations, for advice, consultation and notes for the information contained in this section.

33 See list of potential consultants and suppliers.
34 The authors are grateful to Geoff Wallis CEng MIMechE, Dorothea Restorations, and Robert Jameson, Foster and Pearson Ltd, for advice, consultation and notes for the information contained in this section
35 Wa2.5 and Sa2.5 are visual standards of cleanliness described in British Standard EN ISO 8501.

36 Rusteta Rust Conversion Coating and Corrosion Inhibitor, a 'water based chelating polymer, methoxy propanol, which neutralises the corrosion process by reacting with the iron oxides to form stable and insoluble blue-black metallo-organic complex ready for painting after reaction; forms an excellent adhesion promoter for subsequent coating systems,'

available from Indestructible Paint Ltd (description from Calibre Metalwork through the architect Spence & Dower).
37 Coatings to the metalwork were Rust-oleum Mathys Metal Primer 569, followed by two coats of Rust-oleum Mathys Alkathane 7500 satin finish, supplied by Rust-oleum UK (see list of potential consultants and suppliers).

Bibliography

References

App ASPC Scotland 1814 Appendix to the General Report of the Agricultural State, and Political Circumstances, of Scotland. Edinburgh: Arch Constable and Co

Castagnino, V 2013 *Felton Park Hall Greenhouse, Felton, Northumberland: Chemical Analysis of Window Glass: Technology Report. Research Report Series No. 5-2013*. Swindon: English Heritage

Edgar, J 2011 *The Horticultural Houses in the Upper Garden, Quarry Bank, Styal, Cheshire: The Early 19th-Century Context*. Rodney Melville + Partners

Grundy, J, McCombie, G, Ryder, P, Welfare, H and Pevsner, N 1999 *The Buildings of England: Northumberland*. Harmondsworth: Penguin Books

Henderson, J 1814 'Observations on the Improvement of Hot-Houses &c.', *in* Sinclair, Sir J, *Appendix to the General Report, of the Agricultural State, and Political Circumstances, of Scotland. Drawn up for the consideration of the Board of Agriculture and Internal Improvement*, Vol I. Edinburgh

Loudon, J C 1818 'Letter to the editor'. *New Monthly Magazine and Universal Register*, **IX**, 314

Loudon, J C 1825 *The Green-House Companion; Comprising a General Course of Green-House and Conservatory Practice Throughout the Year*, 2 edn. London: Harding, Triphook and Lepard

Loudon, J C 1833 *An Encyclopaedia of Cottage, Farm and Villa Architecture and Furniture*. London: Longman, Green, Brown and Longmans

Louw, H 1991 'Window-glass making in Britain *c* 1660–*c* 1860 and its architectural impact'. *Construction History*, **7**, 50

McIntosh, C 1838 *The Greenhouse, Hot House, and Stove*. London: Wm S Orr and Co

Repton, H 1805 *Observations on the Theory and Practice of Landscape Gardening*. London: Printed by T Bensley, Bolt Court, for J Taylor, at the Architectural Library, High Holborn

Further reading

Ashurst, J and Ashurst, N 1988 *Practical Building Conservation: Vol 4: Metals*, English Heritage Technical Handbook. Gower Technical Press

Ayrton, M and Shilcock, A 1929 *Wrought Iron and Its Decorative Use*. London: Country Life Ltd

Beaver, P 1970 *The Crystal Palace, 1851–1936*. London: Hugh Evelyn Ltd

Bussell, M 1997 *Appraisal of Existing Iron and Steel Structures*. Ascot: The Steel Construction Institute

Chadwick, G F 1961 *The Works of Sir Joseph Paxton 1803–1865*. London: Architectural Press

English Heritage 2011 *Practical Building Conservation: Timber*. Farnham: Ashgate

English Heritage 2012 *Practical Building Conservation: Glass and Glazing*. Farnham: Ashgate

Gardner, J S 1893 *Ironwork*. London: Chapman & Hall Ltd

Gloag, J and Bridgwater, D 1948 *A History of Cast Iron in Architecture*. George Allen and Unwin Ltd

Harris, J 1960 *English Decorative Ironwork, 1610–1836*. London: Alec Tiranti Ltd

Haudicquer de Blancourt, F (trans 1989) *The Art of Glass*

Kohlmaier, G and Von Sartory, B 1986 *Houses of Glass: A 19th-century Building Type*. Cambridge, MA: MIT Press

Mandel, G 1990 *Wrought Iron*. Leicester: Magna Books

May, W J 1885 *Greenhouse Management for Amateurs*. London: L Upcott Gill

Minter, S 1990 *The Greatest Glass House: The Rainforests Recreated: Royal Botanic Gardens, Kew*. London: HMSO

Robertson, E G and Robertson, J 1977 *Cast Iron Decoration: A World Survey*. London: Thames and Hudson

Rolt, L T C 1970 *Victorian Engineering*. Harmondsworth: Pelican Books, Penguin Press

Speechly, W 1779 *A Treatise on the Culture of the Pineapple and the Management of the Hot-House*. York: A Ward

Sutherland, R J M (ed) 1997 *Studies in the History of Civil Engineering: Vol 9: Structural Iron, 1750–1850*. London: Ashgate Publishing

Thorne, R (ed) 1990 *The Iron Revolution: Architects, Engineers and Structural Innovation 1780–1880: Essays to Accompany an Exhibition at the RIBA Heinz Gallery*. London: Royal Institute of British Architects

List of potential consultants and suppliers

Adshead Ratcliffe & Co Ltd (01773 826661): Arbomast BR, a non-setting, one-part butyl rubber sealant suitable for metal-to-metal contact to exclude moisture on reassembly of joints. Arbomeric MP20 one-part high modulus modified polymer sealant used for glazing in lieu of putty [Swiss Garden]

Antel Perfecting Chemicals (023 9285 6110): Epoxy putty filler [Swiss Garden]

James Brennan, James Brennan Associates, Castle Top Farm, Bow Wood, Lea Bridge, Matlock, Derbyshire DE4 5AB [Hilton Park]

Brockweir Glass, The Old Hall, Brockweir, Chepstow NP16 7NG [Hilton Park]

Calibre Metalwork Ltd, Hazel Knoll Farm, Torkington Road, Hazel Grove, Cheshire SK7 6NW (01614 274603) [Felton Park]

Cheshire Stained Glass, 3 Biddulph Avenue, Stockport SK2 7LH (0161 483 1939) [Felton Park]

Dorothea Restorations, Unit 15, Bristol Vale Trading Estate, Hartcliffe Way, Bristol BS3 5RJ (0845 4780773) [Syon Park]

Eura Conservation Limited, metalwork conservation, Coalport House, High Street, Coalport, Telford, Shropshire TF8 7HZ [Swiss Garden]

James Finlay, historic paint consultant, Burcombe House, Chalford Hill, near Stroud, Gloucestershire GL6 8EN [Hilton Park]

Foster and Pearson Ltd (**Robert Jameson**), Hook Farm, West Chiltington Lane, Billingshurst, West Sussex RH14 9DP (01403 782868)

Indestructible Paint Ltd, 19–25 Pentos Drive, Sparkhill, Birmingham B11 3TA (01217 022485)

Bob Johnson Consulting, Structural Engineer, 10B, Shoplatch, Shrewsbury SY1 1HL [Hilton Park]

Sherwin Williams (formerly W & J Leigh & Co Ltd), Tower Works, Kestor Street, Bolton BL2 2AL (01204 521771) [Hilton Park]

Tim Ratcliffe Associates, Cambrian House, Nantmawr, Oswestry SY10 9HL [Hilton Park]

Rust-oleum UK, 116 Quayside, Newcastle upon Tyne NE1 3DY (02476 717329): A Dutch manufacturer specialising in paints for marine and high exposure locations [Felton Park]

Tatra Glass (01509 413227): Cylinder sheet (broad glass) [Swiss Garden]

Geoff Wallis, GW Conservation, metalwork consultant, Tamar House, 14 Broncksea Road, Bristol BS7 0SE [Hilton Park, Swiss Garden]

Index

Page numbers in **bold** refer to figures and their captions.